THE PREDATORS

THE PREDATORS

Irene E. Cohen

G P PUTNAM'S SONS, NEW YORK

The lion (Panthera leo) inhabits the grasslands
south of the Sahara Desert in Africa, and the
tiny area of the Gir Forest in India. The two
male lions in the picture on the previous page
have their territory in the pastureland at the foot
of Mount Kilimanjaro, Tanzania.

The Komodo dragon on this page is the largest
living lizard, and grows up to 12 feet in length.
It lives on the island of Komodo, a nature
reserve, in the lesser Sunda Islands, Indonesia.
The lizard is endangered because humans cull its
prey species, which are the wild pig and deer.

CONTENTS

A QUARTO BOOK

Published by
G P PUTNAM'S SONS
200 Madison Avenue
New York N.Y. 10016

©Copyright 1978 Quarto Limited
Library of Congress Catalog Card Number: 77-935632
ISBN: 399-11973-6
First published 1978

This book was designed and produced by
Quarto Publishing Limited
13 New Burlington Street
London W1

Phototypeset in Britain by
Filmtype Services Limited, Scarborough
Printed in Hong Kong by
Leefung-Asco Printers Limited

To Ma, Pa and Al.

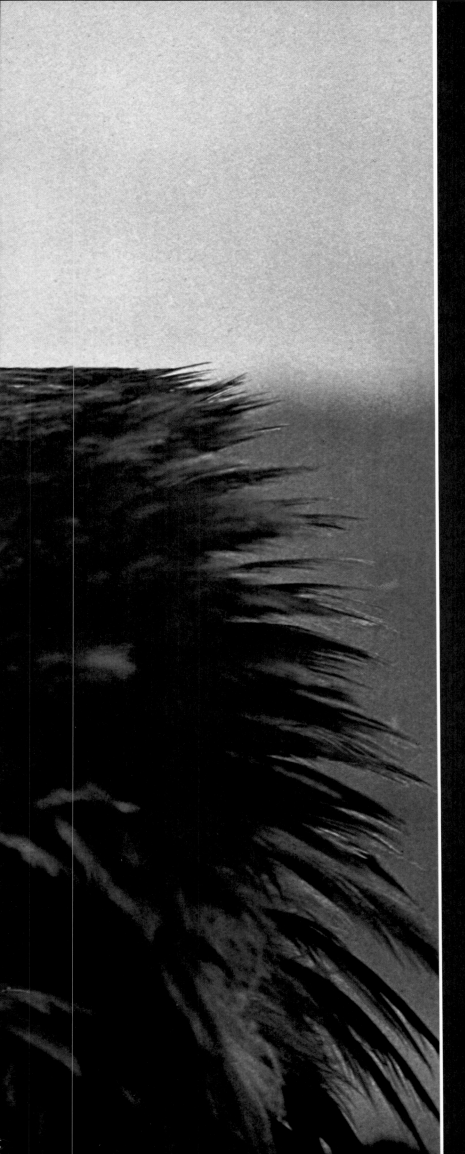

PART ONE

THE FORMIDABLE PREDATOR

From the shrew to the
Killer Whale . . .
its camouflages,
its techniques

Man, himself a predator, has always been fascinated by other predators. The drama that is enacted when one animal violently attacks another in order to provide food for itself and its young is sensational to watch, and it was with mixed fear and admiration that man began to pursue his interest in the many predatory species, in particular the vertebrate ones. It has been found that the methods of predation are numerous. Not all are bloody or dramatic. Many involve only instantaneous, silent gulping. Not all predation is destructive. In fact, it is an essential and constructive pattern in nature. Not all predators are man's natural enemies. They have helped man in many ways. It is possible that imitation of their methods helped to change early man from a roaming herbivore into the most formidable predator of all. Certainly the barbed teeth of certain fishes were imitated in weapons, and the venom of snakes was used to poison arrows. As hunters, haulers, companions, insect eliminators, and the source of many, highly valued products and materials, predators have served man. The vitamins in cod liver are fed to children; feared cobra poison has reduced the pain of leprosy and cancer; and the essential ingredient of adrenaline, found in toad skins and brewed by the Pilgrims into ointment, once helped rheumatic aches and stimulated failing hearts.

The range of habitats to which the members of any species are adapted is reflected in the variety of appearances and forms of behavior shown in that species. However, members of a predatory species, which make their living exclusively by some particular method of predation, are very similar to each other. Individual differences do exist, but, in general, natural selection has drawn the aspect of individuality lightly. Stereotyped behavior and appearance, fundamental to survival, have been etched deeply into the genetic substance. Physiological cycles and rhythms of predation behavior, mechanisms of stimulating and dampening aggression, group behavior, growth and learning are just some of

(Previous page) The Galapagos Hawk survives food scarcity by indiscriminate predation.
(Right) The hunting cheetah may slink through grass cover before the attack.

*The Griffon vulture (*Gyps fulvus*) inhabits barren areas such as mountain steppes and high plateaux. The absence of foliage enables the bird to sight and circle its prey. Vultures depend on accidental death to provide their food. This means that their diet is varied and can consist of anything from the remains of an elephant to the blubber of a whale. When a vulture sights a kill, the maneuvers it makes betray its knowledge to other vultures and they mass at great speed to share the pickings.*

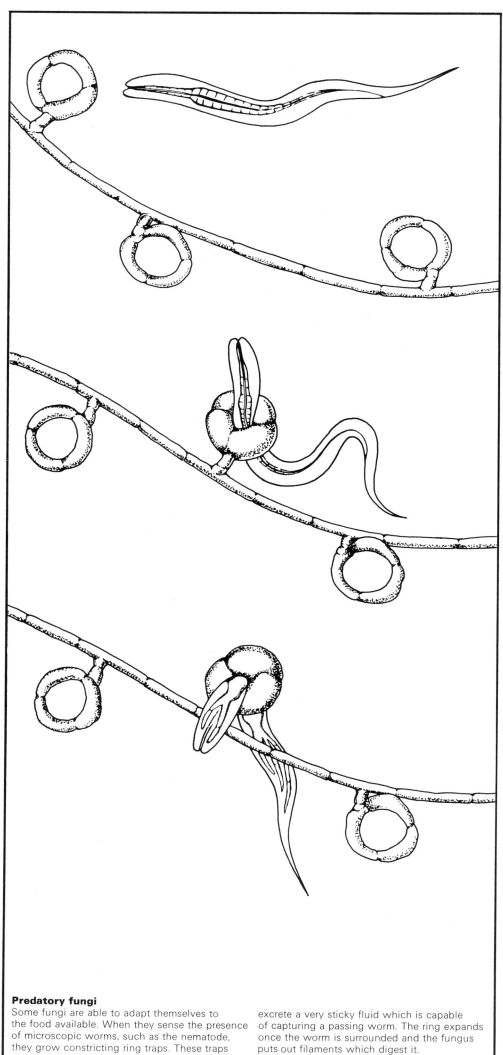

the important biological areas that scientists have uncovered in their researches, and more is learned all the time about the delicate sense organs of the animals, such as ultrasonic detectors and eyes that produce their own light.

In spite of their usefulness, predators frighten man. Their sudden strike in shadowy waters or from behind rocks, their occasional attacks upon children and livestock, the diseases, like rabies that they may carry, have all left an indelible blot of fear on the memory of our species. This has often resulted in the creation of superstition and legend, and a greater understanding of predators and predation can replace fear with respect.

Predation is the regularized pattern in which one species lives by consuming another. It does not include acts of aggression between members of the same species, even if such acts result in the death or consumption of the victim, as occasionally happens with wolves. Predation also does not include acts of defense, even when the defender may succeed in killing or consuming the attacker.

A predator is not precisely the same thing as a cannibal or a carnivore, although cannibalism and carnivorousness are characteristic of predatory species. These species are not limited to mammals. They include certain kinds of carnivorous fishes, lizards, snakes, and birds.

Predators range in size from microscopic to monstrous, from the invisible predatory fungi to the 15,000 pound killer whale. Some are plants with built-in structures that snare their prey just as effectively as the sharp teeth and claws of the more familiar animal predators. For example, the fungus *Trichothecium cystosporium*, a species of bacterial mold, can prey upon microscopic worms, called nematodes. It catches them with sticky secretions or constricting ring traps that appear only when nematodes are available. Otherwise, the fungal predators quietly thrive on decaying matter in the soil. It is quite common for predators to scavenge, when their prey is scarce, but it is very uncommon for them to be able to develop new structures, like the fungus, at the opportune moment. In this respect, man and mold are some-

Predatory fungi
Some fungi are able to adapt themselves to the food available. When they sense the presence of microscopic worms, such as the nematode, they grow constricting ring traps. These traps excrete a very sticky fluid which is capable of capturing a passing worm. The ring expands once the worm is surrounded and the fungus puts out filaments which digest it.

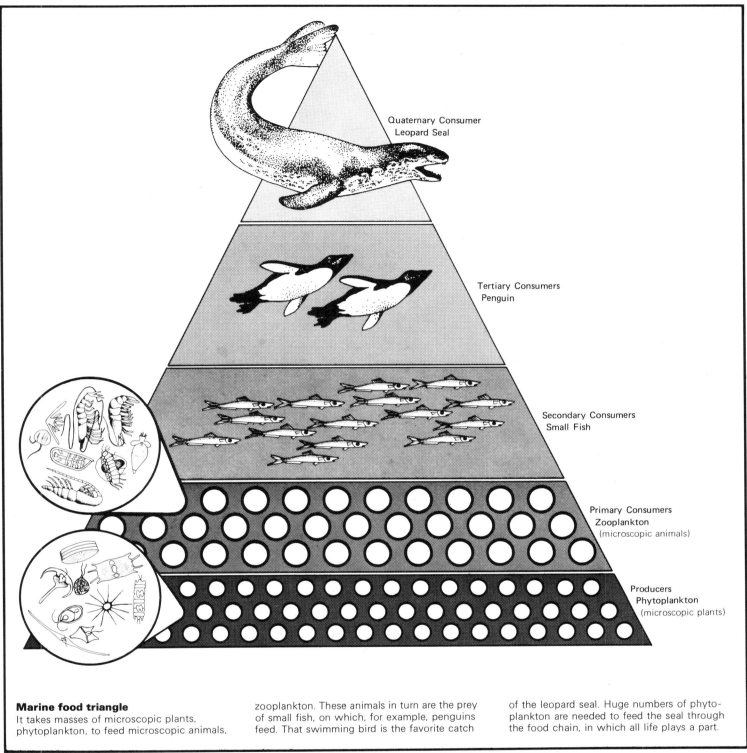

Marine food triangle

It takes masses of microscopic plants, phytoplankton, to feed microscopic animals, zooplankton. These animals in turn are the prey of small fish, on which, for example, penguins feed. That swimming bird is the favorite catch of the leopard seal. Huge numbers of phytoplankton are needed to feed the seal through the food chain, in which all life plays a part.

what alike. Molds grow ring traps to seize worms, and men take up weapons, exogenously changing their structure in order to kill prey.

Predatory fungi are very important in the balance of nature. They consume the worms that would damage the roots of important crops like wheat, potatoes and pineapple. From this example, it is clear that each species is a link in the chain of energy transfer from plant to herbivore to carnivore to bacteria and back to soil and plant again. All predators, large and small, occupy some vital point on this circular chain. All but the largest vertebrate predators may lead a predatory life until the day they become someone else's prey.

Most predators are at the top of the food pyramid. This means they get their sun energy indirectly at third or even fourth hand. Man, who shares the peak of the pyramid with other predators, is omniverous and generally eats primary consumers like cattle or autotrophs. Occasionally, man will eat higher order consumers, such as animals who eat other animals, in other words predators, like snakes, turtles, fish and frogs. However, man rarely eats carnivores such as bears.

Predators insure the balance of the ecosystem by preventing an over-proliferation of primary consumers. If predators did not exist, their prey, the primary consumers, would multiply rapidly and deplete the plant foundation. Old, sick, weak, injured, young and less alert prey are always a predator's first victims. This helps main-

tain the fitness of the prey species by repeatedly eliminating diseased individuals and the carriers of harmful, or at least less helpful, genes. Thus predators are one of the natural selective forces working on prey populations.

This interaction takes place everywhere. It happens at the bottom of polluted, metropolitan ponds and in the icy, arctic oceans, maintaining the vital balance of every ecological zone. Predators, then, should be revered and protected by man, not only for their strength, speed, beauty, ingenuity, and aggressiveness, but for their role in the maintenance of all forms of life. They should be imitated by man, not only in the patience of their stalk and daring of their strike, but also in the economy of their predation.

PART TWO

THE PREDATORS IN THE SEA

In the darkness
of the oceans,
fish evolve super-senses
to help them in the hunt

All life seems to have had its beginning in the sea. Even the most complex modern land forms recall their origin in the salty medium through which they see and the watery environment, internally contained, through which they hear, taste, and gestate their young.

Man, a species young in evolutionary time, has walked this 4·5 billion-year-old earth for only 2·5 million years. In this short existence, which is less than one-thousandth as long as the existence of one-celled algae, for instance, the species has come to contemplate the origin and history of life, which left its first, simple, microscopic imprint on rocks solidified more than 2·5 billion years ago.

In studying the slow transformation from life in the sea to life on land, man discovers his own inheritance. In comparing the behaviors of sea and land predators, man assesses his own predaceousness. Learned predatory behavior, superimposed upon a genetically aggressive potential, seems to be man's legacy. Do other species learn to be predators? Were there always predators?

We know that predation is often learned ontogenetically, but that more frequently predatory behavior is spawned with a creature, as part of its phylogenetic inheritance. If this is so, then who were the first predators and on what did they prey?

In the broadest sense of the word predation, the first heterotrophic, one-celled organisms, which derived nutrition by taking in organic molecules from the primeval soup, were predators. But it was not until the appearance of photosynthesizing autotrophs, that heterotrophic types could be said to be consuming other species. And it was not until heterotrophs began pursuing each other as food, that true predation arose.

Some of the first predatory animals are found in the sparse fossil record of pre-Cambrian seas. There, more than 600 million years ago, all the known invertebrate phyla were already in existence, feeding upon the diversifying algal plant life and upon each other.

The first vertebrate predators were fish. They were the Agnatha, and were

Dolphins leap from the water (previous page) in order to be able to breath.

Scientific classification
Two hundred years ago, Karl von Linné, who became known as Carolus Linnaeus (1707–78), invented a system of classifying and describing all animals and plants. This enabled scientists to communicate more precisely their findings from research. The first and widest classification is of kingdom, which divides plants from animals. The next division, phylum, divides plants and animals into more specialized groups. The animal kingdom is divided into 26 phyla, one of which is Chordata. This group contains all animals that had at some time during their development a notochord, or cartilaginous band forming the basis of the spinal column. Those animals which have a backbone are the sub-phylum with which this chart is concerned. Within this sub-phylum are five classes: fish, amphibians, reptiles, birds and mammals. At one time there was a super-class which referred to those vertebrate animals living on land, but this classification is no longer used. The order and the family further break down the characteristics of animals into ever smaller and more precise groups, and there are inter-classifications within them. The names of the genus and species are linked together to give precise identification, for example, the Basking shark's Latin name, *Cetorhinus maximus*. A species cannot be defined any more precisely than by saying that those animals that mate and breed in the wild and produce fertile offspring are of the same species.

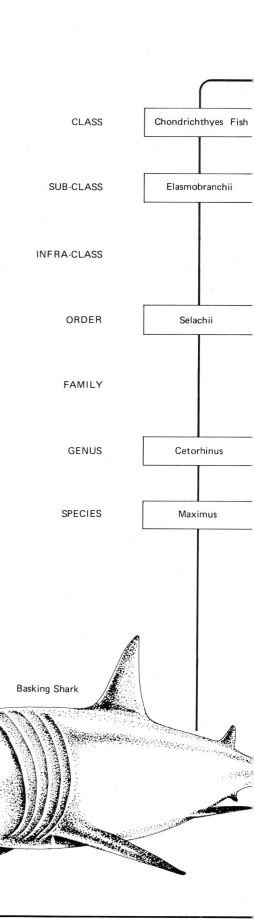

CLASS	Chondrichthyes Fish
SUB-CLASS	Elasmobranchii
INFRA-CLASS	
ORDER	Selachii
FAMILY	
GENUS	Cetorhinus
SPECIES	Maximus

Basking Shark

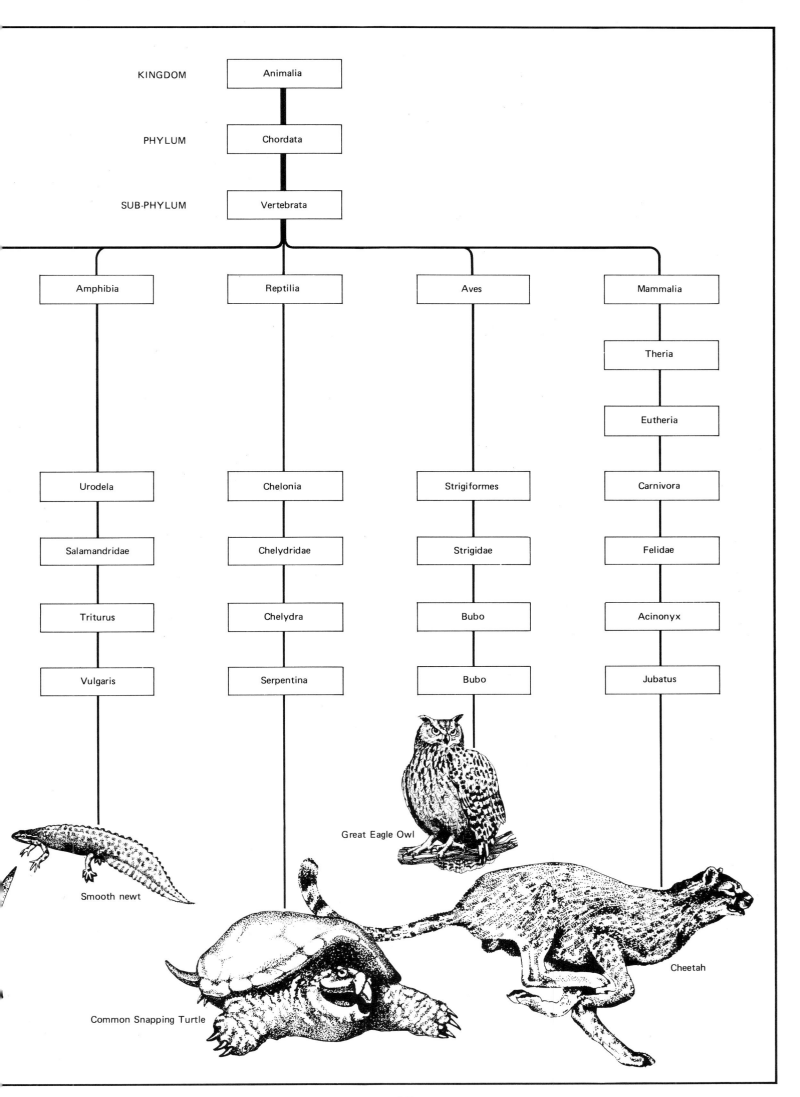

KINGDOM	Animalia		
PHYLUM	Chordata		
SUB-PHYLUM	Vertebrata		

Amphibia	Reptilia	Aves	Mammalia
			Theria
			Eutheria
Urodela	Chelonia	Strigiformes	Carnivora
Salamandridae	Chelydridae	Strigidae	Felidae
Triturus	Chelydra	Bubo	Acinonyx
Vulgaris	Serpentina	Bubo	Jubatus

Smooth newt

Great Eagle Owl

Common Snapping Turtle

Cheetah

17

jawless like their descendants the hag-fish and lamprey eel. Some of the Agnatha gave rise to jawed fish, which were armored with bony plates and had cartilage rather than bone as skeletal material. These were called Chondricthyes and lived 400 million years ago. They were the ancestors of sharks, skates and rays. Others evolved from the jawless progentior into the bony fishes (Osteichthyes), which were the predecessors of 95% of all modern fishes.

From the sea, many fishes moved to freshwaters where they continued to evolve. Some became the first verte-brates to move on land, the amphibians. Many years later some of these return-ed to life in or near the sea like the Marine toad (*Bufo marinus*), and Marine Iguana (*Amblyrhynchus cristatus*). Reptiles evolved from an amphibian ancestor, and although they were better adapted for life on land than their amphibian forebears, they too gave certain species back to the sea. The sea snakes of the genus *Fordonia* and the Leatherback Marine Turtle (*Dermochelys coriacea*) are two examples. They are 'reverse-amphibians.' Instead of living on land and returning to the water to lay eggs, marine reptiles live in water and return to land to lay eggs. In fact, this reproductive requirement has made the leatherback an endangered species.

In Malaya, man has robbed leather-back rookeries consistently for edible eggs. This giant predator, weighing up to 1,200 pounds, with a seven-ridged, black carapace up to six feet in length, swims in temperate waters, until the spawning season, when it returns to the tropics. Eating crustaceans, mol-luscs and small fish, *Dermochelys* grows to be the largest extant turtle. Unfortunately, it soon may be an extinct turtle, if man does not learn to protect it.

During the later Jurassic period, about 150 million years ago, mammals and birds diverged from a common, land reptilian ancestor. Again some species of mammals and birds later adapted to marine existence. Seals, walruses, and whales; penguins, gulls, and pelicans make their predaceous living through the sea.

True caymans (left), crocodiles and alligators have exposed teeth in the lower jaw.

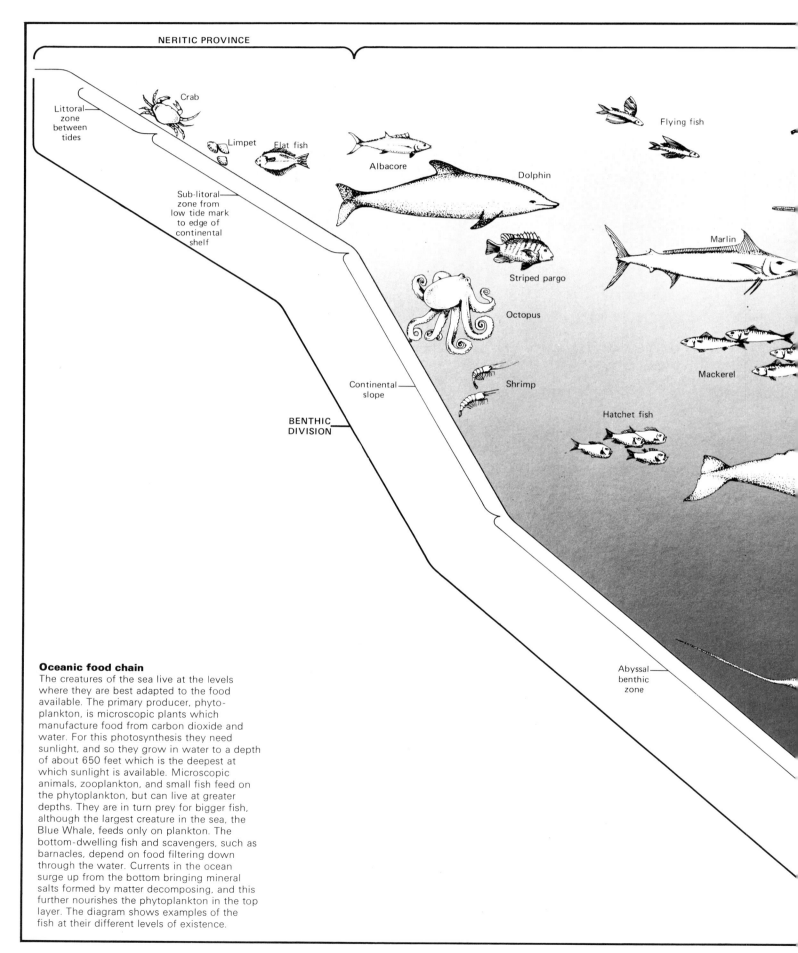

NERITIC PROVINCE

Crab

Littoral
zone
between
tides

Limpet

Flat fish

Albacore

Flying fish

Dolphin

Marlin

Sub-litoral
zone from
low tide mark
to edge of
continental
shelf

Striped pargo

Octopus

Continental
slope

Shrimp

Mackerel

BENTHIC
DIVISION

Hatchet fish

Abyssal
benthic
zone

Oceanic food chain

The creatures of the sea live at the levels
where they are best adapted to the food
available. The primary producer, phytoplankton, is microscopic plants which
manufacture food from carbon dioxide and
water. For this photosynthesis they need
sunlight, and so they grow in water to a depth
of about 650 feet which is the deepest at
which sunlight is available. Microscopic
animals, zooplankton, and small fish feed on
the phytoplankton, but can live at greater
depths. They are in turn prey for bigger fish,
although the largest creature in the sea, the
Blue Whale, feeds only on plankton. The
bottom-dwelling fish and scavengers, such as
barnacles, depend on food filtering down
through the water. Currents in the ocean
surge up from the bottom bringing mineral
salts formed by matter decomposing, and this
further nourishes the phytoplankton in the top
layer. The diagram shows examples of the
fish at their different levels of existence.

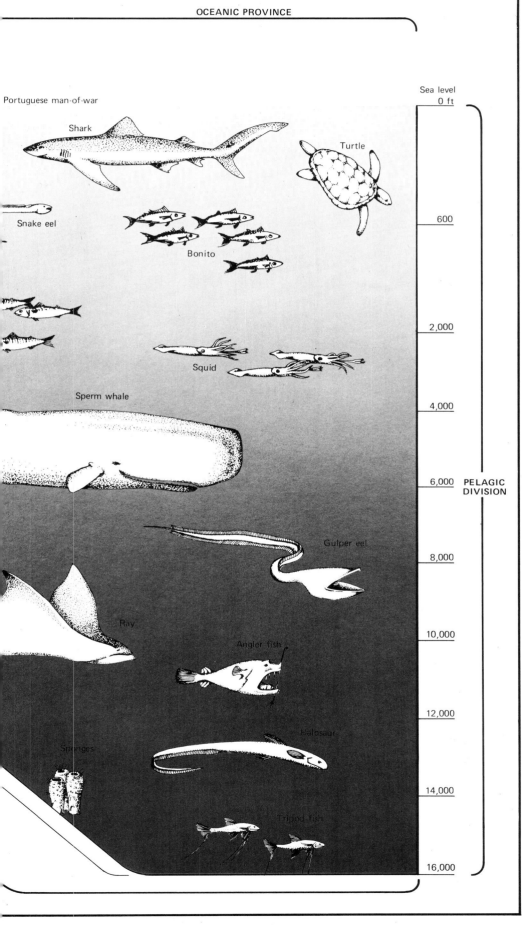

OCEANIC PROVINCE

Sea level
0 ft

Portuguese man-of-war

Shark

Turtle

Snake eel

600

Bonito

2,000

Squid

Sperm whale

4,000

6,000 PELAGIC
DIVISION

Gulper eel

8,000

Ray

10,000

Angler fish

12,000

Halosaur

Sponges

14,000

Tripod fish

16,000

Fish

The greatest number of marine predators belong to the class of Fishes, in particular the bony fishes and the cartilaginous sharks, skates and rays. Many of the fish we eat are also eaten by large fish, like barracuda and shark. Our own predation on sharks has reduced some of the competition from them, but barracuda are less reliable as prey species for us because their flesh is often poisonous.

Each year we kill millions of fish, most of which are predators. Since fish are the oldest class of vertebrates, they have had a vast period of time in which to evolve an enormous number of feeding preferences and adaptations. Fish eat everything from microorganismic plants and animals to invertebrates, like worms, snails, crustaceans and insects, to vertebrates, like other fish, amphibians, reptiles and mammals. In their voracity, some of the larger predatory fish attack and eat inanimate objects including clothing, canned food which is still in the cans, and underwater cables.

There are about 30,000 different species of fish. Since most of these have a predatory function somewhere in the aquatic food chain, only a few can be chosen here to highlight their economic and evolutionary importance.

Apart from the usual predatory adaptations like wide, powerful jaws, predatory fish have an abundance of marvellous lures and weapons. Some of them have paddles, saws, swords or electric stings with which to stun their prey and defend themselves. Some of them have bioluminescent eyes that permit them to search the dark depths for food. Deep water predators are often weak-sighted or blind, and these find their prey by sense organs that pick up mechanical vibrations or electrical pulses in the water. For example, members of the Mormyrid and Gymnotid families send out electrical pulses that establish an electrical field. When the field is crossed by prey or an inanimate object, the fish can detect a change in the field and react.

The reproductive systems of fishes are just as diverse as their predatory adaptations. They range from hermaphroditism and simple oviparity to ovoviparity that shades through many nuances to true viviparity in certain species of sharks.

Bony fishes

The overwhelming majority of marine and fresh water fishes have bony skeletons. They are called, collectively, Teleosti. They range in weight from a fraction of an ounce to hundreds of pounds, and all of them have scales, gills, and gill covers. Most also have bony rays that spread and support their fins.

The multitudes of fish are divided into large taxonomic groups called superfamilies, like Lophiiformes (Angel Fishes) which include 220 species; Pleuronectiformes (Flat Fishes) including about 600 species; and Perciformes (Perch-like Fishes) of which there are thousands of species. There are more than 25 of these superfamilies consisting, in all, of thousands of different predatory fishes, some of which are our favorite eating and sporting fishes.

The Angler Fishes occupy shallow and deep waters from Iceland to the Mediterranean. They include specimens from six to 60 inches long, whose mouths and stomachs expand to accommodate victims, and which all have wiggling lures growing out of their heads, bodies or fins to attract prey.

Two of the benthic species are of particular interest. *Ogcocephalous nasutus*, the Shortnose Batfish, is as unattractive as its name and behaves more like a frog than a fish, having modified pectoral and pelvic fins that it uses to hop along the sea bottom.

Holboell's Deep Sea Angler (*Ceratis holboelli*) has a curious form of sexual dimorphism. The female of the species is 45 inches long, while the male is only half an inch long. The male attaches itself to the body of the female and becomes a sperm-producing organ, which makes the female, in effect, a self-fertilizing hermaphrodite.

Several other species of marine and freshwater fish have hermaphroditic sex glands, including certain basses, perches and salmonoids, but none has the Holboell Angler's unique integration of the male into female organism. The male is like an external embryo, even sharing the same circulatory system with its host.

Other species are sequentially hermaphroditic. That is, they are first one sex, then the other. Some sea basses (*Serranidae*) are protandric (i.e. male first), and the Swordtail (*Xiphophorus helleri*) are protgynic. After the female has spawned several broods, she transforms into a 'sword-bearing' male.

The delicious Dover Sole, flounder, plaice, halibut, and others are all predators of invertebrates and other fishes. They are members of the Flat Fishes superfamily, so named to indicate their body shape and the fact that, by maturity, their mouths and eyes have shifted over to the top surface, while they float with their dark pigmented side toward the bottom. The largest of them *Hippoglossus hippoglossus* (halibut), grows to 80 inches and 160 inches exceptionally.

Other very important commercial fishes, like tunas, cods and herrings, are all predators too. *Thunnus thynnus* gain their unique flavor and large size (up to 1,200 lbs) by eating herring, gar-

The death of the bream supports the life of the bass. Death comes suddenly in the ocean and a catch is speedily consumed.

fish, mackerel, and squid. They swim in warm seas in groups of hundreds, moving, when pursued or pursuing, at speeds over 20 miles per hour.

The Cod group is a large superfamily, including hake, whiting, and cod. Like many other predators, cod (*Gadus morhua*) show a metamorphosis of diet with age. The young eat worms and crustaceans, and the adults eat herring, sand-eels and shoal fish.

The Herring group includes anchovies, sprats, sardines, herring, trout, salmon, and pike. Salmon (*Salmo salar*) grow up to 50 inches long, eating fishes and crustaceans. They are quasi-freshwater, however, having the habit of returning in spring to spawn in the rivers where they were born. On these inland journeys, salmon fast, their main food being far away, and most of them do not survive to return to their feeding grounds in the sea.

Perch-like fishes are also sometimes river spawners and dwellers. Many are edible – pompano, perch, sea bass, swordfish, mackerel – and swim in fast-moving schools. The popular menu fish, *Pomatomus saltatrix* (bluefish), can eat a fish longer than itself. It may grow to 35–40 inches in tropical and temperate seas.

The archer fish (*Toxotes jaculatrix*) is another member of the enormous Perciformes superfamily. It is found in rivers of southern Asia and Australia, where it thrives on fish and invertebrates as well as insects flying above the surface. The mature archer can nab flying prey by accurately spitting a stream of water up to four feet high.

In contrast to the archer, which swims near the surface, bottom-dwellers lurk in the mud, waiting for prey. These are, for example, the species of the Northern Stargazer (genus *Astrosco-*

(Above) A plaice ideally camouflaged in its bed of sand. (Right) The pike is impervious to the barbs of the Tenspined Stickleback.

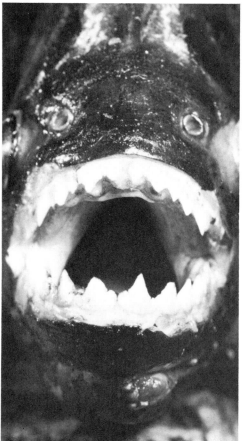

pus), named to indicate the permanent upward fixation of their eyes. Both eyes and nostrils poke up out of the mud, as do its poisonous spines. No defensive or offensive adaptation seems to have escaped the Stargazer for it has a worm-like lure on its lip and a 50-volt electric sense organ as well. No crustacean or small fish in the vicinity would seem to have a chance.

Of fishes with predatory anterior extensions, Perciformes supply two outstanding examples – the Atlantic sailfish (*Istiophorus albicans*) and the swordfish (*Xyphias gladius*). Both of these use their maxillary prolongations to swat, stun and kill prey, which include herring and mackerel.

Some predatory fishes have attacked man. This usually occurs because of some provocation because man is not a species that could be considered a regular link in the marine food chain. It is also true, however, that some of the larger fish are singularly indiscriminate in their choice of foods

when they are hungry (which in many cases is almost always).

The Speckled Moray Eel (*Muraena helena*) is a ferocious nocturnal hunter and member of the Anguilliformes group. These eels can grow to 50 inches in length, and they live in marine shallows. They rely on their sense of smell for hunting and stay coiled near the bottom, waiting for fish and squid. Eels have long been part of human gastronomy, and are reputed to have been fattened on human flesh for royal feasts in classical Rome.

The feared piranhas (*Serrasalmus*) are a South American river species of the great Carp group (Cypriniformes). Normally, they eat other fishes, and it is only by accident that they attack birds or mammals, including man. There are more than 6,000 species of Cypriniformes, and these include the predaceous Electric Eel, with its areas of modified muscle tissue that can deliver stunning 300 volt shocks; and the extraordinary, pelican-mouthed Gulper Eel, which hunts with the assistance of luminescent organs in deep

(Top) the feared piranha normally will eat only other fishes. Its mass of pointed teeth (left) make it an awesome opponent.

waters, to 5,000 feet, around Bermuda.

The other bony fishes most feared by humans belong to the Mugiloids group, including barracudas, mullets, smelts, and rainbowfish.

There are about 18 species of Great Barracuda (*Sphyraena*) in the tropical Atlantic and Pacific. Their ecology and predatory habits have been studied in detail because they are not only dangerous on the rare occasions when they attempt to eat man, but sometimes also when they are eaten by man. Attacks by barracudas can be understood as part of their predatory and defense behaviors, and poisonings caused by eating their flesh, can be understood as the result of a complex exchange of substances between plants and animals.

The barracudas, all members of the Sphyraenidae family, are found in every tropical sea, except the eastern Pacific. In summer, when temperate seas are warmer, they travel as far north as Cape Cod and as far south as Durban. They are popular sport fishes, and are eaten in many parts of the world. Because of their position in a complicated food pyramid that may have at its base toxic blue-green algae, barracudas can become poisonous indirectly. That is, where barracudas feed on fish, that feed on poisonous invertebrates, that feed on toxic algae, the result is a toxic barracuda. In this way, barracuda toxicity is related to the geographical areas where blue-green algae grow on the coral reef.

Toxicity is also related to season. At certain times of the year, barracudas prey on Tetradontiformes, such as triggerfish, puffer and porcupine, which are spawning. During this spawning season, the gonads of the prey species are very poisonous, and barracudas which eat them become toxic. Because it is common to find certain fish toxic during spawning and because only mature barracudas, that are over three feet in length, seemed to be poisonous, it was once thought that the reason for the barracuda's toxicity was its own biochemical, breeding-season changes. However, this appears not to be the correct explanation, since barracuda toxicity outlasts its spawning time.

Other fish are also the recipients of

The barracuda (above and right) is a popular sporting fish, but it becomes poisonous to man if it has recently eaten spawning fish.

chained poisons through their prey. Why then are barracudas poisonous so much more frequently than, for example, amberjack, king mackerel and sea basses? It is probably explained by the fact that barracudas are the best equipped predators. With the sharpest teeth and keenest appetites of all, barracudas eat more of the foods that will make them toxic. This is why the size of the predator is positively related to toxicity. The larger individuals of many of these reef-feeding species are poisonous because they prefer and are strong enough to tackle the large, toxic tetradontiform fishes.

In a perceptive analysis, Donald de Sylva has shown that the correlation of size, geographical location and season to toxicity can all be explained by diet. As the barracuda matures, it moves to deeper waters, eats larger more poisonous prey, and, therefore, is most often poisonous when it is longer than three feet and caught near deep reefs in the spawning season.

Since most people catch young barracudas of eight to ten inches in length, which feed on shoal fishes in the concealment of underwater mangrove roots, the fishermen do not have to fear poisoning. It is only large barracudas, which move out to depths of 200 feet and hunt solitarily for perciformes, mugiloids, and tetradontiformes, that should not be eaten.

Barracudas rely on sight to obtain their prey. They are hungriest in the daytime, especially in the morning. Their stomachs usually contain one type of fish depending on availability. For instance, in the waters off New Caledonia they may eat mullet; off Singapore, anchovies; off Australian coasts, garfish.

Barracudas are attracted to injured, struggling fish. Many spearfishermen have been startled by a barracuda that darts in to steal their catch, dashing off with fish and spear. Because of this innate attraction to the flashing iridescence of erratically moving fish, a shiny ring, bracelet or wristwatch worn by a swimmer might stimulate a barracuda attack. Without such unconscious provocation, barracudas almost never attack people. When injured, or hunting at dusk, a barracuda may mistake a human being for its normal prey.

Cartilaginous Fishes

Barracudas do not compete with sharks, although they occupy some of the same waters. Sharks generally eat larger prey than barracuda, and are much more likely to attack humans, given the opportunity.

Long viewed as the villains of the sea, sharks are extremely numerous and various in their descriptions. Like all dangerous predators, they serve a vital function in maintaining the balance of their ecosystem.

Sharks belong to the class of cartilaginous fishes, along with skates and rays. They have plied the oceans and inland seas for over 300 million years, and marine scientists are just beginning to learn the adaptive lessons embodied in their behavior and anatomy. Silurian ancestors of modern sharks lived in freshwaters, and are 200 times older than all other classes of vertebrates. About 340 million years before the formation of the Rockies and the Himalayan mountain range, ancient sharks descended to the sea, where they remained small in numbers, until Jurassic times, 180–135 million years ago. Then they flourished into many families, including the 'flattened sharks' or skates and rays. By Miocene times (25–10 million years ago), when the common ancestor of monkeys, apes and man seems to have first appeared, every extant species of shark, from dogfish to whale shark, was already plentiful.

Many fossilized shark teeth were found in limestone deposits at sites throughout the United States of America. Although many of these sites are now landlocked, they were once covered by ocean. If it were not for these fossils, little would be known about shark ancestry, because cartilage skeletons do not fossilize well. From the teeth, the species and size of the individual can be determined. For instance, a six-inch tooth found at the site of the now dry Temblor Sea, near Bakersfield, California, suggests that the Great White Shark (*Carcharodon carcharias*) had a Miocene ancestor whose average length was 80 feet. Even today it appears there are sharks of tremendous size, because dredgers

Not all sharks are man-eaters, but this Australian Grey Nurse Shark is ferocious and its appetite for swimmers is well known.

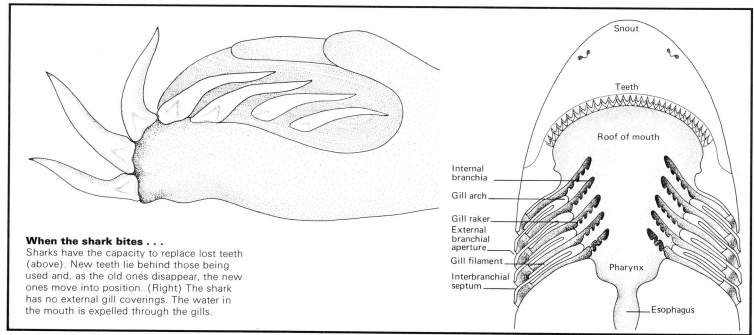

When the shark bites . . .
Sharks have the capacity to replace lost teeth (above). New teeth lie behind those being used and, as the old ones disappear, the new ones move into position. (Right) The shark has no external gill coverings. The water in the mouth is expelled through the gills.

Snout

Teeth

Roof of mouth

Internal branchia

Gill arch

Gill raker
External branchial aperture

Gill filament

Interbranchial septum

Pharynx

Esophagus

have brought up modern shark teeth that are four inches long. In fact, the largest living fish is a shark, *Rhincodon typus* (whale shark), which may grow to 60 feet in length.

Although several courageous researchers have been tagging, filming and observing sharks for two decades, much more remains to be learned about the shark (Selachii). New species are often reported. In 1976, 35 miles north-east of Hawaii, a 14·5 foot long 1,650 pound specimen hooked its huge mouth onto the anchor of a Navy torpedo recovery ship. It suffocated at 500 feet and was hoisted aboard and dubbed *Megamouth*. It looks very much like the 13 foot, 1,200 pound Tiger Shark (*Galeocerdo cuvieri*) which has a jaw span of more than 40 inches, and is capable of swallowing a man.

The fact that *Megamouth* suffocated under 500 feet of water may seem puzzling at first. After all, fish are supposed to be able to breathe under water. Sharks, like bony fishes, can use their gills to take oxygen from the water, but certain species of sharks do not have strong muscular activity to widen the gill arch angle and permit water to enter the richly vascularized gill clefts for gaseous exchange. These species, such as mackerel shark (*Lamna nasus*), depend on swimming to force sufficient water through the gills. When in captivity or bound under water, these sharks become sluggish and may even die. Aquarium keepers some-

times 'take them for walks,' that is, drag them around shallow pools, until they revive. In addition, sharks do not have air bladders, like so many of the Teleosti. Air bladders can be used as supplementary organs of respiration and to help keep the fish afloat. Without air bladders or strong respiratory musculature, the sharks must keep swimming to avoid sinking and suffocating.

There are more than 25 different species of sharks, ranging in size from less than three inches (*Squaliolus laticaudus*) to more than 45 feet (*Rhino-*

codon typus). But there are certain general characteristics that all Selachians share. Unlike bony fishes, sharks have non-socketed teeth, a ventrally, rather than anteriorly placed mouth, and an asymmetrical tail, with the vertebral column continuing into the longer, upper lobe.

The fins of sharks, prized for oriental soups, are fleshier than those of Teleosts, which have bony rays that support and spread their fins. In male sharks, the pelvic fins conceal paired appendages, called 'claspers', which deposit seminal fluid in the female

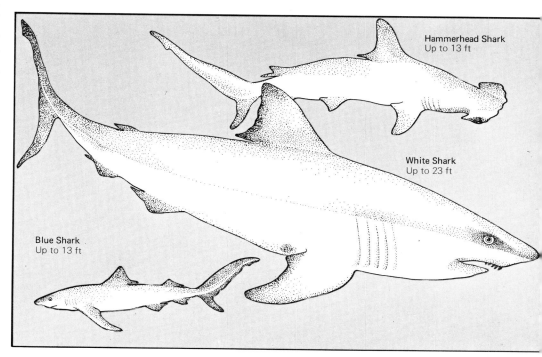

Hammerhead Shark
Up to 13 ft

White Shark
Up to 23 ft

Blue Shark
Up to 13 ft

This 13-foot White Pointer Shark weighed 1,139 pounds and was caught off Queensland.

by millions of denticles or preformed (undifferentiated) teeth. Denticles range from the microscopic to the clearly visible and painfully palpable. Each one is a true tooth with central pulp and dentine. The abrasive skin of certain sharks has long been used by carpenters as a fine sanding tool, and by sharks themselves to lacerate their victims with a lash of the tail.

The sense upon which sharks most rely to find their prey is olfaction. The limits of their sense of smell cannot be measured accurately, but it is estimated that sharks can detect odors at distances greater than two miles. The nostrils serve no respiratory function but are devoted exclusively to the sense of smell. When water enters them, dissolved elements are picked up by nerve receptors connected to the olfactory lobes, which form the greater part of a shark's brain.

Vision is a much less powerful sense than smell. The eyes are important, however, when the shark is near its prey. Like so many nocturnal and dark-habituated species, the eyes of deep-water sharks are equipped with a light-reflecting layer of cells behind the retina, called the tapetum, that intensifies dim underwater light. There is also a nictitating (winking) membrane that blinks up to cleanse the eyes.

Sharks employ hearing and 'distant touch' to track down prey. Professor Warren Wisby of the University of

during copulation. All sharks reproduce by intercourse which sets them apart from almost all other fish, in which eggs are externally fertilized. The insemination takes about twenty minutes and results in deposition of eggs (oviparity), or in litters of live-born young, which have been nourished on yolk and developed in the oviducts of the mother (ovoviparity), or which have been nourished by a combination of yolk and nutrient exchange by means of a placenta (viviparity).

Shark offspring are fully-equipped predators at birth. Some say their predaceousness can be expressed even before birth, since sharks sometimes attack each other in the womb. Their equipment includes a variety of sensory organs for locating prey, denticled skin, and numerous sharp, replaceable teeth.

Sharks have classic predaceous teeth which are not socketed in the jaw, as in other vertebrates, and often become loose when the shark bites. Fortunately for the shark, these teeth are easily regrown from the skin which is covered

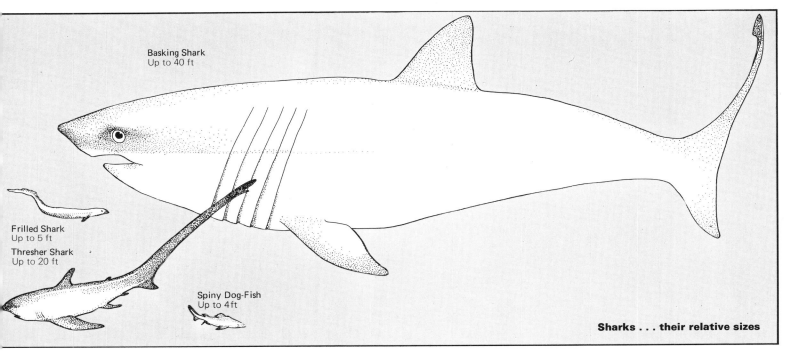

Basking Shark
Up to 40 ft

Frilled Shark
Up to 5 ft

Thresher Shark
Up to 20 ft

Spiny Dog-Fish
Up to 4 ft

Sharks . . . their relative sizes

Miami has studied the ability of sharks to detect high and low frequency vibrations. He used conditioning experiments, in which small electric shocks were coupled with sounds of particular pitch, to discern the keenness of hearing in his shark subjects. He knew when a shark heard a certain sound by observing the messages delivered from electrodes attached near the shark's heart. If the shark heard a sound that had been repeatedly associated with shock its heart would skip a beat. In addition to sound hearing, or what humans perceive as sound, sharks detect very low frequency vibrations that travel at about 5,000 feet per second. Professor Wisby called this the sense of 'distant touch,' and it is mediated by nerve tunnels on the head, jaw and along the length of the body. Picking up these vibrations brings the shark within 100 feet of its prey, at which point hearing and vision are of greater assistance.

Once the victim has been caught and killed, it is generally digested very quickly. This is a feature common to many carnivores, whose strong gastric juices break down meat and bone. The hydrochloric acid in shark stomachs is strong enough to eventually dissolve metal objects also. The stomach leads into a spiral valve intestine that further processes the food and absorbs nutrients. The resulting faeces are spiral-shaped and are often found as fossils called coprolites. As long ago as 1671, Claude Perrault drew an accurate diagram of the shark's spiral valve intestine.

Sharks are by nature fish eaters and do not depend on human flesh for their survival. The Leopard Shark (above), which rarely exceeds 8 feet in length, is harmless to man. The Tiger Shark (left) is more ferocious, and has been known to attack swimmers.

The largest family of sharks is Carcharlinidae or Requiem Sharks. The Brown or Sandbar Shark (*Eulamia milberti*) is a member of this family and the one most commonly sighted among bathers off the coast of the north-east and mid-Atlantic States of America. They grow to about 61 feet and weigh approximately 100 pounds. Their brownish or light grey backs are often seen as they cross sandbars off Long Island Beaches. In summer they meander into New York Port and bays. They may even surprise the gondoliers on the canals of Venice. The United States' West Coast Brown Shark (*Apristurus brunneus*) is a different species and a member of a different family. It is much smaller than *E. milberti* and inhabits deep water from Alaska to southern California.

Although the Brown Sharks do not have as great a reputation for voracity as other species, no shark's potential should be ignored. Elisabeth Keiffer states that the jaws of an eight foot long shark can exert a force of 20 tons per square inch compared with our own of several hundred pounds per square inch, and the orangutan's several thousand pounds per square inch.

In contrast, there are many documented reports of attacks on man by the tiger shark (*Galeocerdo cuvieri*). Its rapacity is known throughout the world, from South Africa to the Gulf of Mexico to the Philippines. Amazingly, a native pearl diver in the Torres Straits, between New Guinea and Australia, survived an attack by a tiger shark. He had a tooth imbedded in his neck, which led to positive identification of the species.

Perhaps the worst aspect of occasional shark predation upon man is the fact that species that normally live in the open seas or oceans often enter rivers where they find little food. Consequently they become extremely vicious towards completely unsuspecting people.

In the Karun River, near Ahwaz, Iran, 27 people were attacked between 1941 and 1949. British army records show that half the attacks were fatal, and some occurred in one foot of water. Sharks are common in the warm rivers of Australia, India, and the Middle East. Large numbers of them have even been reported as far as 30

miles up the Delaware River in the United States of America. They may also invade the colder inland waters of Maine and Canada.

The shark's ability to penetrate hundreds of miles into freshwater systems, and to adapt itself to less salt in the water, interests scientists because it may have something to do with the presence of urea in the shark's tissues. Physiologists would like to find out how sharks can tolerate urine constituents in their blood because this might give them a clue to solving the fatal uremia problem that occurs in human beings who have malfunctioning kidneys.

Since sharks do not find as much food in rivers as in the sea, why do they come to freshwater at all? Eugenie Clark found an explanation in her study of reef sharks, which seem to benefit from freshwater vacations because the clear water loosens the grip of parasites attached to their skin. Certainly they do not come in pursuit of prey or to attack children playing and swimming in rivers, although this has occurred when a spawning, lost, or hungry shark strikes out.

More often it is the man who pursues the shark with intent to consume, instead of the reverse. Selachian cuisine is proof of man's long-standing, and well-planned predation on sharks, skates and rays. The Soupfin Shark (*Galeorhinus zyopterus*) is sought for its Vitamin A rich liver oil as much as for its fins. More than 17 million pounds of dogfish (sharks of several species: *Squalus canthias*; *Scyllium canicula*; *Scyllium catulus* and others) are caught annually for English markets, where they are disguised with more palatable names, like 'rock salmon' and 'huss.'

Although many countries are ashamed of their appetite for these fish, and refuse to call a shark a shark or report their catches of these species to the United Nations' survey of food fish, sharks are very nutritious and popular. One pound of dogfish supplies more protein and energy than the same weight of eggs, milk, lobster, or salmon. Furthermore, there are no dangerous bones to swallow. Dogfishes (of the family Triakidae) teem in the spring and summer waters off New York, New Jersey and southern New England. This resource, that could pro-

vide vital protein for millions of malnourished people, is largely ignored by powerful nations seeking to provide aid. This is probably because these countries fall in the Judeo-Christian sphere of influence, where prejudice against shark-eating stems from a Biblical injunction, in Leviticus 11: 9–12, against eating scaleless fishes. This prohibition by no means applies universally, and many people eat Selachians without any queasiness. The conversion of shark meat to 'flour' will probably prove the best method of integrating this high-protein food into the diet of many nations.

The normal diet of sharks is other fish, squid and octopus. Perhaps this is why their own flesh forms such an ideal concentration of protein. The Sand Sharks (*Carchorias arenarius*), which are not to be confused with Sandbar Sharks, prefer schools of flat and bluefish. Sometimes a number of sharks surround a school of one of these fish and attack in unison. The sand shark is much feared as a mankiller in Australian waters, and, although it has a less fearsome reputation in American waters, records exist of at least one attack on a skin-diver in Long Island Sound.

The 30- to 40-foot Great White Shark (*Carcharodon carcharias*) probably is the most voracious species. It strikes with the mighty impact of its 7,000 pounds and can tear chunks out of small wooden craft with its two-inch-long, serrated, triangular teeth. An entire horse was found in the stomach of one Great White. They have also eaten sea turtles, seals, and even a thirsty elephant which ran into the coastal waters off Kenya. But like most sharks, the Great White likes to eat fellow Selachians as much as it likes to eat everything else. Two sharks, six to seven feet long, were found in the belly of one Great White.

The Hammerhead Shark (species of *Sphyrna*) particularly like the taste of sting-rays, and consume them avidly despite the poisonous barb. Tiger Sharks are notoriously cannibalistic and are often found with the remains of various species of shark in their stomachs.

The appetites of sharks are so formidable that they present vigorous competition to man's own predation

on many fish species. Thresher Sharks (*Alopias vulpinus* and *Alopias pelagicus*), for example, eat mackerel, bluefish, shad, bonito, and herring. They use the long blade of their tail like a scythe to kill prey, and they sometimes cooperate with swordfish to kill big whales.

The Canadian Department of Fisheries mounted a razor-edged ram on the hull of a ship to kill Basking Sharks (*Certorhinus maximus*) which eat the same plankton-type food as the salmon and cod fished in the northern waters. The basking sharks had been harrassing the fishermen by destroying nets and traps and by leaping out of the water near fishing boats. One of these leaps, which are performed supposedly to rid the sharks' skin of blood-sucking parasites like the sea lamprey, capsized a small vessel in a three-storey back-splash, killing the crew. The danger associated with this leaping habit can be appreciable, considering that a big basking shark may weigh 8,000 pounds.

But these are not the largest sharks. The longest sharks and largest known fish are Whale Sharks (*Rhincodon typus*). Their average length is 32 feet and they may grow exceptionally to 60 feet. One caught off the Florida Keys weighed 26,594 pounds. Two fishing boats and the crews took seven hours to land a five-ton specimen at Magalore, India.

Although they are the largest, whale sharks are less aggressive than other species. They are sluggish and are often rammed by ships as they leisurely feed on tiny fish and crustaceans. Unlike most other species of sharks, they are oviparous and lay their enormous egg cases in the deep, tropical waters of the Atlantic, Pacific, and Indian Oceans.

The smooth Dogfishes (*Mustelus canis*) are five feet or less, but they are so numerous in certain seasons that they make a large dent in the fish species we prey upon. In the waters off the eastern coast of North America, 10,000 of them can eat as many as

When the Tiger Shark (above) opens its jaws it shows several rows of serrated teeth. It produces and sheds 24,000 teeth in 10 years.

60,000 lobsters, 20,000 crabs, and 70,000 other fish in a year. These rapacious sharks have blunt teeth that crush shellfish, and they have the ability to protect themselves from enemies by changing their skin color from pearl to dark gray.

But who or what could be the enemy of such accomplished predators? Man is their first enemy. Although sharks are extremely tenacious of life, even when injured, they are very vulnerable to injury at the gills and to being hoisted head down.

Apart from man, the principle enemies of sharks are other sharks, and occasionally swordfish (*Xiphias gladius*) and killer whales (*Orcinus orca*) will attack them. Little is known about confrontations between top predators, but the discovery of a 110 pound swordfish inside a 600 pound Mako Shark (*Isurus oxyrhynchus*) shows that either adversary may win.

Mammals of the sea

It certainly seems unnecessary to resort to imaginary tales of sea monsters in order to be inspired by marine fauna. Especially when we look at whales, dolphins, and porpoises, we find in reality the material of myths. The marine mammals include many species that have extraordinary size and intelligence. They are all predators, some eating tiny plankton animals and some eating large vertebrates like sharks, seals, and other cetaceans.

Whales and their relatives, known as cetaceans, were land animals once. Although there are few fossil links between the land ancestors and their marine descendants, the skeletal anatomy of cetaceans strongly suggests that evolutionary change remodelled the parts that had originally permitted animals to leave the aquatic environment. The earliest fossil whales are dated at about 40 million years ago. The ancestor that gave rise to them and the cloven-hooved land animals probably lived 200 million years ago.

Cetaceans have no legs, but rudimentary pelvic bones support reproductive organs. Occasionally a whaling station report contains pictures or photographs of a whale with imperfectly formed hindlimbs. V. B. Scheffer tells of a Humpback Whale (*Megaptera novaeangliae*), killed near Vancouver, which had aberrant legs more than a yard long. The forelimbs of cetaceans contain the basic skeletal elements of land-dwellers' forelimbs. The forelimb flippers and the two horizontal tail flukes assist in swimming and steering. The flukes are made of strong fibrous tissues and have no bony supports.

The cetacean skin is smooth and sensitive, and, like pigs, they generally wear a frozen but genial smile on their lips. Hair, that is typical of all mammals, has been replaced by an insulating layer of blubber that conserves warmth just as hair or fur would. Like all mammals, cetaceans are warm-blooded and maintain a constant body temperature. The firm-packed tissue network that supports blubber can range from one inch in depth in porpoises to one foot in blue whales. It maintains homeothermy in cold seas.

Blubber is such an effective insulator that it retains the heat produced as a dead whale decomposes. When the whale is cut open, the muscle tissue under the blubber is cooked.

Besides staying warm, cetaceans must solve the problem of keeping cool. When they dive, leap, and swim quickly, their muscles produce heat which cannot be dissipated by sweating or panting. The circulation system of whales, therefore, carries warm blood to the undersurface of the skin where it can be cooled by the water. There are also capillary nets, called *retia mirabilia*, that seem to serve as reservoirs of oxygenated blood to nourish vital organs during long, deep dives, when blood pressure and heart rate are depressed.

One of the largest cetaceans is the Giant Sperm Whale (*Physeter catodon*). It may grow to 60 feet and weigh 26,500 pounds. As much as $3\frac{1}{2}$ tons of plankton can be eaten daily by a growing *Physeter*, but adults settle into a more modest diet of a ton and a half per day.

Giant sperm whales like to congregate in groups of 1,000 or so, hunting together for squid and fish at intermediate and deep sea levels. But *Physeter* is small compared to the largest living organism, the Blue Whale (*Balaenoptera musculus*), which may grow to 100 feet and weigh up to 80,000 pounds.

The Blue Whale's focus of predation is on zooplankton and small crustaceans of many species. These mammals and other, large, plankton-feeders are gentle sea-grazers which inhabit northern and temperate seas in spring and summer, and migrate to deep tropical waters in autumn and winter for breeding. They feed by straining seawater through nine to ten feet long brushes of whalebone (baleen) that hang like hairy draperies from the 'palate' or upper jaw. A two-ton mouthful of water causes the long creases (rorquals) on the whale's underside to expand. When the rorquals contract, water is forced out of the mouth, and the food remains inside. Their food is found relatively close to the surface, so baleen whales do not

A Killer Whale opens its ferocious jaw. It will attack even the larger baleens.

34

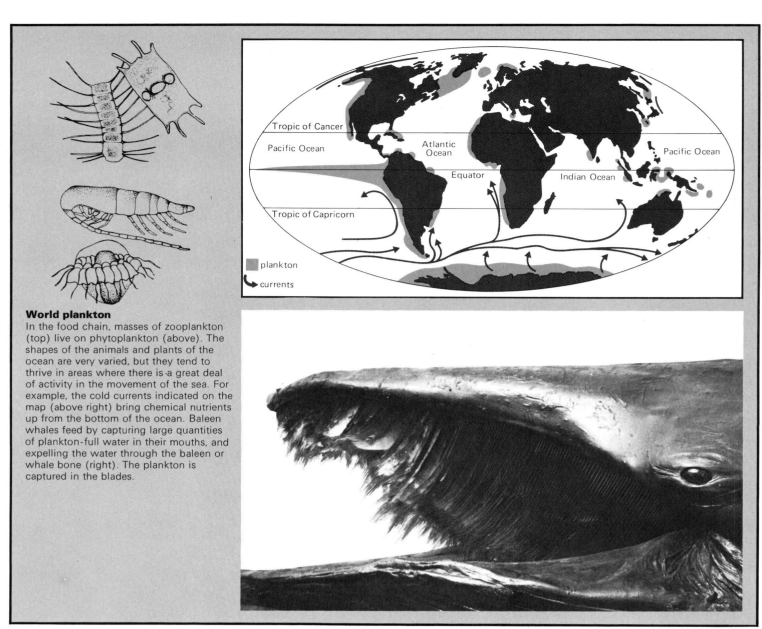

World plankton

In the food chain, masses of zooplankton (top) live on phytoplankton (above). The shapes of the animals and plants of the ocean are very varied, but they tend to thrive in areas where there is a great deal of activity in the movement of the sea. For example, the cold currents indicated on the map (above right) bring chemical nutrients up from the bottom of the ocean. Baleen whales feed by capturing large quantities of plankton-full water in their mouths, and expelling the water through the baleen or whale bone (right). The plankton is captured in the blades.

Tropic of Cancer
Pacific Ocean
Atlantic Ocean
Pacific Ocean
Equator
Indian Ocean
Tropic of Capricorn

plankton
currents

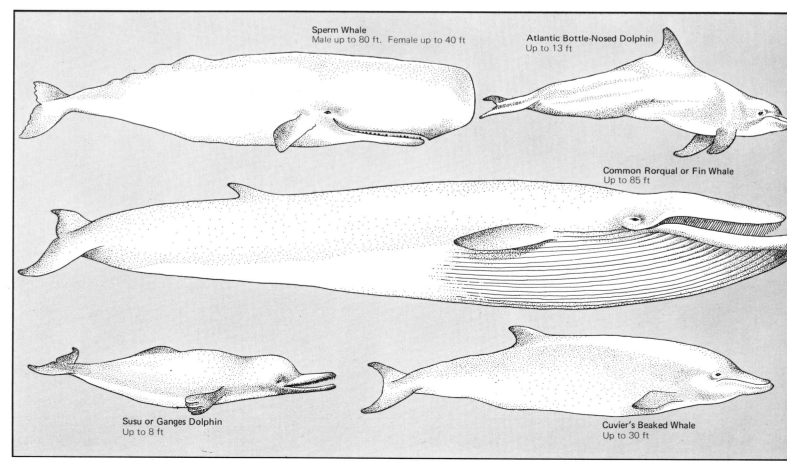

Sperm Whale
Male up to 80 ft. Female up to 40 ft

Atlantic Bottle-Nosed Dolphin
Up to 13 ft

Common Rorqual or Fin Whale
Up to 85 ft

Susu or Ganges Dolphin
Up to 8 ft

Cuvier's Beaked Whale
Up to 30 ft

dive below 325 feet. However, other large whales make very deep dives, that may last up to two hours, to eat such delicacies as giant squid and deep water fish.

Physiologists are still trying to understand the adaptations that permit whales to cope with all the physical problems entailed in deep diving and rapid returns to the surface. When human divers come up too quickly, the dissolved nitrogen in their blood forms gas bubbles that can block blood flow in blood vessels that feed the brain and other organs.

Whales do not suffer this painful syndrome, called 'the bends,' apparently because they take down only a certain amount of air in their lungs, in order to limit the amount of nitrogen that can dissolve in the bloodstream. Naturally, their great size means they have also much more blood in which to dissolve this nitrogen. Excess air, forced out of the lungs at tremendous depths, is trapped in the convoluted sinuses off the windpipe. The foam of oils and water in the sinuses seems to hold the nitrogen until it can be expelled in the blowhole spout.

The cetaceans are divided into two suborders: the Odontoceti or toothed-cetaceans and the Mysticeti or filter-feeders. The giant Sperm Whale belongs to the former and the huge Blue Whale to the latter.

One of the families of Odontoceti, called Monodontidae, contains two unusual creatures. These are the Narwhal (*Monodon monceras*), probably the source of the unicorn legend, and the pure white Beluga Whale (*Delphinopterus leucas*). The mature narwhal male has an 8- to 9-foot spiralling horn growing out of its snout. Aside from making life more dangerous for the hunted narwhal, scientists cannot explain what the horn does. It does not seem to participate in predation, or in breaking through ice to enable the narwhal to get to the surface and breathe. Since it is a strictly sexually dimorphic feature, it may have something to do with group defense or mating. Perhaps the female narwhal finds it irresistibly charming.

The Monodontidae are medium-

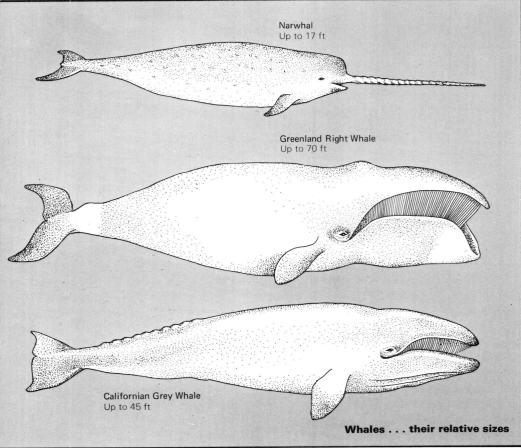

Narwhal
Up to 17 ft

Greenland Right Whale
Up to 70 ft

Californian Grey Whale
Up to 45 ft

Whales . . . their relative sizes

The Fin Whale or common rorqual (above) is one of the main targets of whalers now that the Blue Whale is nearly extinct.

sized as far as cetaceans go. They are usually 17 to 18 feet at maturity and weigh about 1,000 pounds. They are gregarious and inhabit cold circumpolar waters, where they eat crustaceans and fish.

The other members of the Monodontidae family, the beluga or white whales, are the 'polar bears' of the marine mammals. The adults are completely white and their bodies form an almost perfect spindle shape. They are normally found in the open sea, in the Arctic Ocean, Bering and Okhotsk Seas, but sometimes stray into large Canadian, Alaskan, Siberian, or Norwegian rivers. One lost Beluga was reported in the Rhine about ten miles from Bonn, in 1966, and another was spotted off Ile de Bois near Nantes in 1948.

Delphinidae is another Odontoceti family. It contains two of the best

(Above right) A Fin Whale in the Sea of Cortez, Mexico, swims close to a ship. (Above right) Southern Right baleen whales in a mating chase. (Below) Fin Whales seen swimming through Lerwick Harbor, Shetland, Scotland.

adapted marine predators, the Bottle-nosed Dolphin (*Tursiops truncatus*) and the Killer Whale (*Orcinus orca*).

Tursiops, like all dolphins, is clever and travels in schools. These dolphins have been observed cooperating in the capture of large numbers of small fish, by pushing waves onto the California Gulf Coast shore and thus trapping their prey in shallow pools.

Killer Whales are not the largest whales, but they are the most ferocious. They attack and eat squid, seals, walruses, narwhals, dolphins, and even the giant baleens.

Although man's fear has permitted him to misinterpret the Killer Whale's ferocity and to massacre the species by the hundreds, some brave people have befriended and studied this predator. Jacques Cousteau and his Calypso crew have observed the Killer Whale in its natural habitat, and Ted Griffin, director of the Seattle Marine Zoo, tamed one, named Namu, which ate 400 pounds of salmon per day.

The Killer and False Killer Whale (*Pseudorca crassidens*) are docile in captivity and have never attacked their keepers. Griffin even rode on Namu's back, signalling it to dive by patting the dorsal fin, which can grow to a height of six feet in certain individuals.

Killer Whales appreciate physical contact and verbal praise. They are said to be more intelligent than dolphins and show this brightness in many ways. Travelling in schools, they hunt cooperatively for seals, penguins, squid, and baleens. Like other intelligent creatures, they are curious and occasionally take time out from hunting to pop their heads above the water and investigate a passing ship. When confronted with the toothy smile of *Orcinus* and the bumping of its big frame

against their boats, men have mistaken inquisitiveness for aggression.

The female Killer is similarly intelligent. She circles her calf protectively, and speaks to it in distinctive clicking sounds. A captive *Pseudorca* female was able to learn tricks taught to the other occupants of her pool, just by watching them. It seems that whales and porpoises grow so bored in captivity that they participate eagerly in nonsensical routines that human trainers demand to entertain crowds.

Killer Whales can be trained with praise alone; no food rewards are necessary. They enjoy gentle words and soft music. Some individuals in captivity have shown their appreciation of a guitar concert by listening attentively and then appreciatively spraying the musician with light foam from their blowhole.

Their mating patterns are also sensitive, with mutual sliding and play preceding the ventral-ventral copulatory act. Gestation lasts 13–16 months, and the young are suckled for one year.

The most poignant proof of Killer Whale intelligence and sensitivity comes from reports of their communication with each other at the time of capture. Namu, Griffin's Killer Whale was followed by its school after it was netted at the mouth of the Bella Coole

(Left) The Beluga Whale. (Above) Namu, the captive Killer Whale, sends up spray.

River. The whales did not attack the boat or their captive companion. A few of them whistled to Namu, but it did not try to escape. The netted whale did not eat for a week after capture and died after one year in the aquarium.

Albert Falco, who worked with Cousteau, played tapes to two female Killer Whales in the California Marine World Aquarium. The sounds on the tapes recorded the dialogue between the whales at the time of their capture. Both females seemed excited by what they heard and swam around their pool quickly, always returning to the loudspeaker, where they replied to the tapes in characteristic trills and clicks.

The language of cetaceans is not well understood either in its content or mechanics. Like other species of mammals that hunt under water or at night, most whales and dolphins can find each other and avoid obstacles in the dark. Unlike fish, which maneuver according to the information picked up by tactile or olfactory senses, cetaceans rely on hearing most of all. Both their language and mobility are dependent on sonar emissions and bouncing sounds off other objects, which is known as 'echolocation.'

We have known, for almost 40 years, that dolphins can avoid nets by reflecting sound off the mesh and the adhering bubbles. Almost immediately after this was discovered, the potential reconnoitering value of this cetacean ability was recognized by the navy. Thousands of research dollars have gone into experiments testing the rules of cetacean speech and hearing.

Speech, in this case, consists of very intense, brief (10 to 24 thousandths of a second) bursts of sound that are sent out in a straight beam. The animal seems to scan its environment with this beam of high intensity sound by swinging its head from side to side. The sounds are probably not produced by the larynx, but at the point of the nasal plug in one of the windpipe passageways. When these sounds hit objects in their path, the echoes produced reveal the size, shape and speed of the 'heard' object.

Hearing, in cetaceans, is sometimes at much higher frequencies than human ears can appreciate, and seems not to occur through their ears but via the bones of the jaw and through the melon-shaped forehead. The ear openings of whales and dolphins are often small, covered with skin or plugged with capsules of bone.

The auditory high frequency limits of cetaceans can exceed our own ten times. The echolocation mechanism is sensitive enough to permit dolphins (*Tursiops truncatus*) to distinguish between a piece of fish and a waterfilled decoy, and between metal sheets of different thicknesses. The Sperm Whale uses echolocation to hunt squid 500 fathoms below the surface and can perceive prey up to 1,200 feet away.

(Top) The gentle touch of a 3,000 pound Killer Whale. (Right) Bottle-nosed Dolphins. (Left) A captive Dolphin leaps from his pool.

PART THREE

THE PREDATORS IN THE AIR

Their grace in strike,
precision of attack,
and economy
of predation

When they appeared, birds and mammals, like all new life forms, existed on the periphery of a strong and elaborate ongoing biological dynasty. Just as fish appeared against the thriving diversity of plant and invertebrate animal life in the sea, and amphibians first developed as a specialized branch of the fish hegemony, so birds and mammals evolved from different variants of a few of the many hundreds of reptile species prevalent during the Jurassic period. At that time, about 160 to 170 million years ago, when dinosaurs lived on land and other reptiles had become adapted to marine and aerial life, a few of the first avian and mammalian skeletons were sealed in the fossil record.

How the first attempts at flight were made can only be guessed at. Two American scientists have suggested the cursorial and the arborial theories. According to the former, the early, bird type ran along the ground and developed flight as an accessory to this form of locomotion. According to the latter theory, the ancestors of modern birds lived in trees and evolved the anatomical capacity to cling to branches and the ability to jump and hop on two feet, before their descendants developed the ability to fly.

By Eocene times (about 60 million years ago) most of the extant genera of birds had evolved. At the same time the class of Mammals was expanding on land and had already differentiated into many orders.

Naturally, the class of Birds provides us with the most examples of aerial predation, but other classes of vertebrates also have evolved certain species of predators that can fly.

Among fish there are many types that leap occasionally to avoid nets or underwater predators. When hooked, some game fish like tarpon (*Megalops*) and sailfish (*Istiophorus*) can leap up to 40 feet. But soaring flight for the purposes of escape, snatching of insect prey or for display was developed only among marine flying fishes (family Exocoetidae) and flying gunards (Dactylopteridae) and among two freshwater groups in South America and Africa. With their elongated pectoral fins, they can glide for over ten seconds,

(Previous page) White pelicans flock together in huge numbers at fishing grounds.

covering more than 300 feet, but these aerial expeditions do not seem to be important in their pursuit of animal food.

Among reptiles there are arboreal snakes that can glide from branch to branch by flattening their abdomen. They keep their body in an S-curve and steer with their tail, while in the air. There are species in India (*Chrysopelea ornata*) and in the East Indies (*C. paradisi*). The Indian variety is black and gold and may grow to eight feet; the Malayan type averages about three feet. One of the purposes of their flight is to assist them to catch their prey of small lizards.

Among mammals, there are flying squirrels and 'lemurs,' and certain primates, such as some species of monkeys and apes, which leap, swing and propel themselves through the air exceedingly well, but they do not usually do this in pursuit of animal prey.

Although they are not a familiar sight, there are many species of flying squirrels. The most common type in temperate deciduous forest is *Glaucomys volans*. These squirrels glide between trees, using wide folds of skin stretched taught between hind and forelimbs. In south-eastern Asia species of the Giant Flying Squirrel (*Petaurista*) can glide up to 150 feet and turn in mid-air. Although squirrels are primarily herbivores, they will often supplement their diets with eggs and nestlings.

The flying lemurs are not really lemurs, which are members of the primate order. They belong to a tiny mammalian order, called Dermoptera, consisting of just two species of the genus *Cynocephalus* found in the tropical rain forests of south-eastern Asia. Like flying squirrels, the flying lemurs are principally herbivorous and glide from tree to tree on stretched skin.

The 'flying' primates can make tremendous leaps, using elongated hindlimbs for hopping, as the prosimian *Tarsius* does or using elongated forelimbs for swinging from branch to branch, as the spider monkey (*Ateles*) and the ape *Hylobates* do. Most primates are not predators, however, and a discussion of instances of predation among primates, that is the mammalian order containing man, will follow.

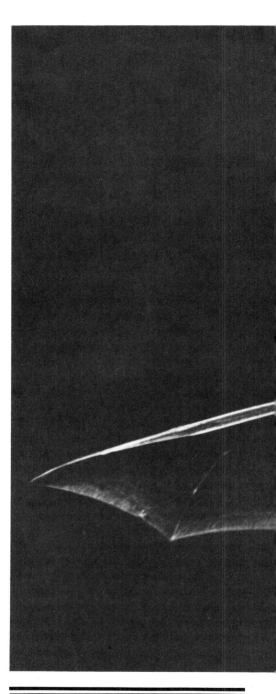

Bats

The principal aerial mammalian predators are bats. These creatures first appeared in late Cretaceous or early Paleocene times, about 65 to 70 million years ago. Why some early insectivorous mammals became adapted to flying is not known, but by Eocene times, approximately 50 million years ago, bats similar to existing species were present. The modern order is divided into Megachiroptera and Microchiroptera.

Most of the 853 species of these small, flying mammals are insectivor-

Bechsteins Bat. Bats are the only mammals to have achieved powered flight.

ous. This diet in bats has resulted in a form of navigation based on extremely sophisticated sound location, which is important among predators of other mammalian orders and possibly among fish-eating bats and birds also.

The apparent silence of the sea and the cave are examples of man's perceptual limitations. The sea is filled with sounds, such as shrimps snapping, porpoises clicking, whales singing, and fish grunting. The cave, like the depths of oceans, is dark and noisy. Dark environments necessitate reliance on senses other than vision. This is why animals of such conspicuously different appearances and lifestyles as the bat

and the blind river dolphin (*Platanista gangetica*) both use echolocation to help them move about and find prey.

Although the chiropteran inhabitants of caves make noises at frequencies that human ears often cannot hear, the sounds are actually extremely loud. The loudness dimension of sound is called its intensity and is measured in dynes/cm^2. The intensity of bat sound is between one and 20 dynes, the latter intensity being about as loud as a jet engine at close range. Considering that bats may roost in colonies of thousands and even millions of individuals in remote caves in Texas and New Mexico, we are truly for-

tunate that the needs of bats are best served by the production of sounds at frequencies inaudible to our ears.

The high frequency nature of the sound pulses produced by bats is well suited to the location of tiny insect prey. This is because a high-pitched sound is produced by a short wave that can be directed at and reflected off a short creature like a moth, with accuracy.

Interestingly, some moths, of the families Noctuidae, Geometridae and Arctiidae, have ears on either side of their thorax, that pick up ultrasonic

bat pulses. When the prey hears the approaching predator, it dives into an evasive flight pattern. Some moths are even capable of emitting ultrasonic clicks, produced by special timbal organs which turn off the bat pursuit, possibly by jamming the bat's echolocating signals, or by indicating to the bat that this particular type of moth is unpalatable.

However, it should not appear that bat diet is limited to moths. Predatory bats eat all sorts of insects, small mammals, birds, nocturnal reptiles and fish. Some bats, for example, the vampire bat, Desmodontidae, exist on blood alone, but since they do not kill their prey for consumption, they are not predators according to the given definition. Many bats will even migrate long distances, like the whales and sharks, to find suitable prey and weather conditions.

Using the sense receptors in their muscles and ears, bats can move swiftly through winding caverns and among branches in the darkest forest without collision. Their maneuverability, although extraordinary, is not infallible, and new obstacles placed in old pathways may be bumped. Also, when tired or just awakened, bat dexterity may be slightly reduced. When they are most alert, however, bats swerve and scoop insects into their wings filling their stomachs with up to 5,000 gnats or 66 moths in a night.

That these nocturnal creatures are helpless without their hearing and vocal apparatus has been known since

(Far left) A Lesser Horseshoe Bat locates the trees and foliage and finds its way between. Bats scoop insects into their wings and the Serotine Bat (left) has settled to consume an Eyed Hawk Moth. (Above) Greater Horseshoe Bats sleeping during the day suspended upside down in a cave.

1793, when Lazarro Spallanzani showed that blind bats retained maneuverability but deaf bats did not. About 150 years later, Donald Griffin showed that echolocation by high frequency, rapidly repeated pulses was the basis of bat navigation. Man uses the same technique to locate underwater obstacles by reading back echoes of reflected sounds on an oscilloscope. This method is called sound navigation, and ranging or sonar. Bats, dolphins, whales, porpoises, seals, and certain birds used sonar millions of years before man first appeared in the fossil record.

A closely coordinated set of anatomical properties permits bats to take prey in flight. Their wings, which consist of skin stretched over elongated finger bones and anchored at the foot, permit excellent gliding control and

African Fruit Bats which have become almost indistinguishable from the leaves on the tree where they hang during their daytime sleep.

immediate response to changes in air currents. Their enlarged collarbones, certain fused vertebrae, large thorax, heart, and lungs are all adaptations for flight.

Many of the bat species also have tremendous external ears that catch sound. The fleshy piece in front of the

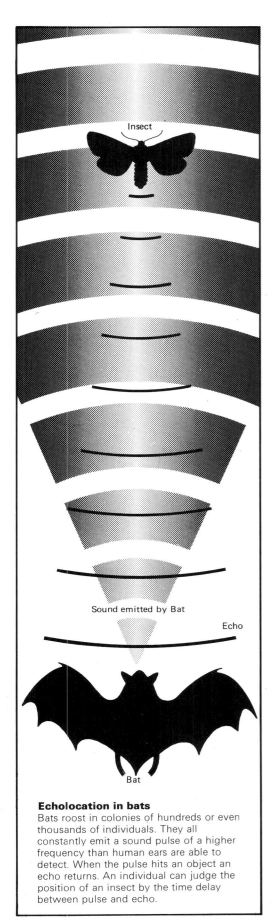

Echolocation in bats
Bats roost in colonies of hundreds or even thousands of individuals. They all constantly emit a sound pulse of a higher frequency than human ears are able to detect. When the pulse hits an object an echo returns. An individual can judge the position of an insect by the time delay between pulse and echo.

auditory opening, called the tragus, is also elongated for sound-funneling. Some bats have elaborate fleshy formations around the nose, mouth, or chin. These bizarre, leafy extensions, as seen on the muzzles of some insect-eating bats, probably direct the sounds emitted from nostrils or mouth toward a a general area.

In total, these adaptations, plus extensive auditory areas in the brain,

give bats the ability to differentiate between the minute echoes that help them distinguish branches, walls, types of prey and other bats in a fraction of a second. The high resolving power of their ears and the rapidity with which they translate sound cue to action is difficult to imagine. Echoes received from sounds that last only 1/100 to 1/1,000 of a second must be instantaneously processed through the brain which directs the next wing movement accordingly.

The average bat sound pulse is 50,000 vibrations per second. At take-off the repetition of the pulse is about 10 each second, and while in flight, it is about 50 each second. How fluctuations in pulse duration or pitch are used in particular terrains or for particular prey is not well understood.

The fact that stands out as most remarkable about the gregarious, echo-locating bats is that they can hear the echoes produced by the sounds they emit, even while they and other bats around them continue to emit ultra-sonic pulses. Even supposing each individual has its own wavelength, bats would seem to have extraordinary auditory discrimination to sort out their particular reflected sound in what must be a continuous racket. Some of the confusion is reduced, however, because ultrasonic sounds die away quickly and the bursts of sound emitted are very short, thus reducing overlap interference.

D. R. Griffin explored and compared the different characteristics of bat voices, trying to determine whether or not the nocturnal fishing bat (*Noctilio leporinus*), and related species (*N. labialis*, *Dirias albiventer*, *Pizonyx vivesi*) can utilize echolocation across the air-water interface. Sitting in his dug-out canoe on the Chagres River in Panama, Griffin observed bats locating underwater prey with precision, even at night over mist-covered waters. He recorded the pulses that seemed to have been directed down toward the water by the fleshy lips. The average pulse lasted five milliseconds and ranged between 28–38 kilocycles at 20–60 dynes/cm². This means that the sounds were very brief, high pitched and incredibly intense or loud. They were directed toward the water at close range, as the bats flew near the surface,

so that in spite of almost total reflection of the pulses, Griffin estimated that enough sound penetrated and reappeared as an echo from the water to permit location of fish. The enormous intensity of the pulses probably compensates for the damping effect of water on sound.

Another problem with sonar 'sighting' of fish from the air is that fish, being composed largely of water, are so like the medium surrounding them that they should be echo-invisible. Most fish, however, have a swim bladder containing air that could provide a good surface for sound reflection.

In any case, the fishing bats do locate their prey, whether in rippled or calm water, whether in rivers, streams, marshes, ponds or coastal waters. When they do sight prey, their large feet with recurved claws dip under the water and land the fish. *Noctilio*'s built-in fishing spears have procured it 30–40 small fish per night, under laboratory conditions. The fish are brought back to the roost in cheek pouches.

During the day, bats sleep in hollow trees, caves, deserted buildings, old birds' nests and even porcupine furrows. Some species can construct a little shelter for themselves by creasing a palm frond and slipping under the tent thus formed. Fishing bats can also shield themselves from light by huddling under their wings, which extend up to two feet when spread.

Roosting communally affords bats some protection from their predator, the large-mouthed Bat Hawk (*Machaerhamphus alcinus*), which can swallow them whole without pausing in flight. Like most predators, this bird will not fly into a large cluster of prey, but waits to pick off the isolated individual. Bats do exude a pungent odor that may deter reptilian predators. Arboreal snakes will occasionally take a roosting bat, and ground snakes, as well as invertebrates, will snap up any ill or young bat that falls to the floor of the cave. At the twilit entrance of a cave, bats can be taken by owls. From their perches, owls watch for exiting bats. Since owl droppings contain the remains of bat bones, it is clear that the excellent twilight vision and hearing of the owl permit it to catch even this swift prey.

Birds

Fossils of the most ancient bird-like reptiles are found in Jurassic deposits 160–170 million years old. Like the bats, whose mammalian ancestor was emerging during the same period, birds made their first appearance at the height of the age of dinosaurs. By Eocene times, about 60 million years ago, most modern genera of birds had evolved.

There are, today, approximately 8,600 species of birds, divided into about 170 families. Unlike the other classes of vertebrates (fish, amphibians, reptiles, mammals), the vast majority of avian species feed on other animals, not plants. This means there are thousands of different kinds of predators in the class of birds. A large proportion of these eat insects and small invertebrates. Some birds of prey, however, are strong enough to take larger prey, such as other birds, rodents, amphibians, reptiles, fish, bats, young antelope, sloths, cats, monkeys, pigs, or lambs.

Understandably, the variety of feeding styles is as diverse as the menu. Delicate Darwin's Finches (*Camorhynchus pallidus*) use a thorn or small twig to scratch insect prey out of bark. The Tohwee (*Piplio*) scratches the underbrush with its tiny claws, looking for invertebrates, while the European Robin (*Turdus*) relies on pigs, bears or men to turn the soil and expose insect delicacies. Birds often behave opportunistically where food is concerned. Some species learn to flock to brush fires that flush rodents out of the woods.

The shellfish-eating birds have evolved or learned ways to extract their prey from their calcified outer coverings. The European Song Thrush (*Turdus ericetorum*) eats snails in winter time, when other underground foods are difficult to obtain, by breaking the shells on hard surfaces. Herring Gulls (*Larus argentatus*) take all foods that are too hard to crush with the bill and drop them from a height onto rocks or hard ground. Parking lots near beaches are often covered with shattered clam shells, dropped by clam-hungry gulls. N. Tinbergen, in 1974, found that this clever tactic will be tried on all hard objects of suitable dimensions, including wooden eggs. It is the hardness of the object, not its edibility, that seems to release the dropping behavior. The European Eagle or Lammergeier (*Gypaetus barbatus*) sometimes follows the same routine, but with a tortoise instead of a clam. Pliny's *Natural History* reports that this eagle habit caused Aeschylus' pre-ordained death. It had been prophesied that Aeschylus would die on a particular day, when a house would fall upon his head. Logically, Aeschylus always spent that day, each year, out of doors. When he was having his fresh-air day one year, a Lammergeier dashed a turtle on his bald pate, presumably mistaking his head for a rock. Aeschylus died, as was foretold, the victim of a house falling upon his head, albeit a turtle's house.

Fishing birds
There are many birds which make fish their staple food. They are usually long-billed, with the edges of the mandible serrated for gripping the slippery fish. Pelicans (species *Pelecanus*), penguins (species *Aptenodytes*), ospreys (*Pandion haliaëtus*), bald eagles (*Haliaeëtus leucocephalus*), flamingos (species *Phoenicopterus*), herons (for example, *Ardea herodius*) and kingfishers

The Osprey (above left) builds its nest high in a
tree on a platform of twigs. It glides above water
and brings its claws forward to attack the fish.
The catch is consumed in a safe place on dry
land (centre left) or given to chicks (below left).
The Fish Eagle (above) and the heron (right)
are both fish-eaters. The heron has a permanent
S-shape in its neck because of the uneven
development of the vertebrae.

from 54 to 72 inches in full span and that flap laboriously to carry off a fish that weighs as little as two to three pounds.

The feathers of osprey are tough and oily, protecting the bird from spray and salt. American Indian folklore states that this oily substance on the feathers attracts fish.

The large nests that ospreys build are surpassed in size only by the eagle's eyrie. They are often several feet in diameter and sometimes provide shelter for the nests of smaller birds that are built below or beside them. The nests are placed in dead trees, on rocky cliffs or sand dunes, even in the crossbars of telephone poles. They are lined with soft seaweed, leaves and plant debris. Ospreys are cautious householders, making sure their homes are in good repair and reinforcing the nest with fresh sticks before going on southward migrations in winter.

Like so many of the birds of prey, ospreys are helpful to man, but unlike most of their raptorial cousins, ospreys are welcome on farms. Their presence insures that other bird-eating hawks will stay away, and since ospreys eat fish, they do not threaten any of the farmers' livestock.

(species *Megaceryle*) are just some of the birds which like to eat fish. All of them have behavior patterns and anatomical specializations that assist them in catching and digesting fish.

Herons and kingfishers wade in shallow waters, then quietly stalk the sighted prey. When within striking distance, they dart out their long necks and seize the fish in the bill. One heron (*Butorides virescons*) was reportedly able to learn to fish by recovering pieces of floating bait used by visitors who came to feed the fish in a park. Using its bill, the heron would gently place a piece of bait on the water surface and watch intently for the nibble of a fish. After catching and swallowing its prey, the bird carefully retrieved the pellet to keep it dry for future use.

A kingfisher may scan the water from above, as well as in the shallows. When it sees its prey, it dives down under the water and takes the fish back to the perch. There the bird grabs the fish's tail and stuns it by slamming its head on a branch. It then quickly turns the fish around and swallows it, head first.

Ospreys and bald eagles both have sharp, deeply curved talons, with rough undersurfaces on the toes to help them grasp their prey. The osprey is the better fisher, and the bald eagle often charges the even-tempered osprey in mid-air, stealing its dead or dying fish.

The osprey is also called the 'fish hawk' and it is ideally suited to flying over large bodies of water and taking

aquatic prey, such as fish, water snakes, and salamanders. The fish it takes are not very economically important to man. They include suckers, horned pouts, carp and bream.

The sharp, black talons, which ospreys use like pincers are very effective fishing spears, but sometimes they sink into a fish that is too large for the bird to carry aloft, and, while struggling to release the fish from its own deadly grasp, the osprey is dragged under and drowns. This does not happen often, and usually the ambitious bird can release its prey. When it is successful, the prize is winged back to the nest, with the fish's head turned forward to reduce air resistance. The osprey has strong wings that range

Kingfishers (left) feed on fish and are found near lakes and streams in Europe, Asia, Africa and New Guinea. Pelicans (above) are the only birds with all four toes webbed, and they have a pouch in which to hold their fish catch. Elegant terns (right) are smaller than royal terns and nest together in large numbers.

Owls

Some of the most persecuted birds of prey have been owls. Because an owl will occasionally take a game bird or domestic fowl and because a great cloak of superstition is wrapped about this order (Strigiformes), owls have been hunted. They are shot by ignorant men who are frightened by the owl calls in the night, and whose teeth are too weak to consume the flesh of the owl once it is killed.

Owls are nocturnal or crepuscular (active at dusk and dawn). A few of them hunt during the day. They are all quiet and stealthy in their habits, with specially adapted, fluffy feathers for whisper-soft flight. With infrared equipment for observation of owls in the dark, Roger Payne observed a keen-sighted owl gliding noiselessly toward a mouse. As the owl floats down to its quarry, its feet are pressed back against its tail. When it is above the victim, the owl simultaneously throws back its head and brings its talons forward. Upon seizing its prey, the owl raises its wings vertically to counteract the extra weight and then ascends to its perch.

In 1949, H. Räber found that the Tawny Owl (*Strix aluco*) recognizes small mammal prey by the movement of the prey as well as its size, while small birds can be recognized by their shape alone. This is because small rodents are active at night, but birds sleep in their nests or on the perch.

Payne's infrared observations confirmed that the movement of small mammalian prey is necessary to direct the owl's attack. As the predator can not always see its victim scurrying in the underbrush, the owl relies on its hearing to pick up the rustling of the mouse or rat. When the floor of a darkened laboratory is covered with leaves and grass, the owl will even swoop on a wad of paper dragged through the artificial underbrush. If, however, the floor is covered with a substance like sand that deadens the

The Tawny Owl (Strix aluco) is the most common owl in Europe. It favors wooded land, and will perch in a tree until it swoops silently down onto small mammalian prey. It has adapted well to town life, changing its diet to birds. The young owl on the right has been brought a small field mouse. Both owl parents care for their young.

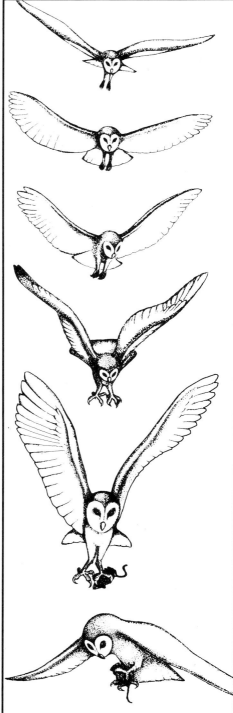

A precision movement

Owls depend a great deal on hearing to locate prey. Experiments have shown that a rustle in leaves and undergrowth will be loud enough to attract a hunting bird, but a mouse on a sand covered floor will be sufficiently quiet to avoid capture. The action of the owl's wings helps it to secure the mouse in its claws (below). It will swoop silently down from a tree, but as it draws near the prey it will flap its wings. This action causes its body to rock forwards and backwards, the feet swing accordingly, and at the final moment the owl will push out its claws and the prey is impaled.

noise of moving prey, the owl can miss or not react at all.

Some prey animals, like the kangaroo rat, have special auditory modifications that permit them to detect low frequency sounds, like the whir of owl wings. Although we are focusing on the abilities and adaptations of predators, it should not be supposed that prey are defenseless or lacking in strength and ingenuity. In the darkness, the ears of both predators and prey are alert. Owls have the advantage of very large auditory openings, asymmetrically positioned to permit maximum sound catching.

Besides the owls, there are other nocturnal birds, such as nightjars, petrels, shearwaters, bat hawks, nocturnal parrots and the fairy penguin. They rely on hearing and excellent night vision. The retinas of nocturnal birds are richly coated with rod cells (56,000/mm) that make discrimination of light and dark, shades of grey and black, extremely acute. The enlarged cornea and lens of the owl's eye help produce a brighter retinal image, and these special features combine to make

owl visual acuity about ten times as great as our own. Owl eyes are so large, and in the case of Eagle Owls (*Bubo bubo*) even larger than man's eyes, that there is little space left in the skull for eye musculature or brain tissue. Instead of swivelling the eye around in its socket, owls swivel their heads to widen the visual field, rotating the skull up to 200° around and even inverting it completely.

Owl eyes have held a special fascination for man. Peering out of the darkness, reflecting ambient light off the densely coated retinas, in shades of red, gold, and green, the eyes of owls were said to produce their own light. These birds can see best the long red and yellow wavelengths of the spectrum and may even be able to detect some infrared waves, but they do not produce their own light. The only animals whose eyes produce light and act as helpful little torches in hunting for crustaceans are certain berycid fishes. The light is produced by glands containing luminescent bacteria.

Like many primates, owls have frontally oriented eyes. This anterior

position of both eyes means that the fields of vision of each eye overlap and provide good depth perception. Binocular vision has evolved separately in anthropoid primates and birds. It is an adaptation to living in trees, where accurate judgment of distance between branches is vitally important. This is an example of parallel evolution. It is a feature which has developed in distantly related species as a response to similar environmental exigencies.

Owl eyes are protected by a nictating membrane (in man this is a vestigial pink membrane located at the inner corner of the eye). The Great Horned Owl (*Bubo virginianus*) uses its nictating membrane when it catches skunks to shield its eyes from the irritating fumes that are its prey's defense. Like all birds, except perhaps geese, owls can not smell, so they are not bothered by the odor that deters other skunk predators. Similarly, the bat hawk is completely undisturbed by the noxious vapors radiated by its favorite food. The great horned owl is the most rapacious owl. It is the only one of its family that can com-

pete with man for prey. Fearless and voracious, the great horned owl has given all owls a bad name in certain places. No other bird of prey, except the Goshawk (*Accipiter gentilis*) and Cooper's Hawk (*Accipiter cooperii*), will go for game birds and chickens, turkeys and guinea fowl as often as this owl does. Sometimes it will even attack large prey like a dog, cat, or other species of owl or eagle, and it may eat only the brains of these larger animals.

This bird is powerfully built, like other serious predators. Its wings spread up to five feet and it is characterized by woodland camouflage feathers of mottled brown, yellow, and black. The female is larger than the male, but the adaptive advantage of this dimorphism has yet to be explained.

The eyes of the great horned owl are deep yellow and vigilant for small prey as well as large. Woodchucks, minks, skunks, weasels, shrews, moles, rats, rabbits, squirrels, mice, and opossums succumb to the eight-taloned force. Since great horned owls rarely establish themselves near human settle-

Owls and their prey. A Barn Owl entering a barn (far left) with food for its young. An Eagle Owl firmly holding down a rabbit (above left). (Top) A Little Owl with a modest earthworm. (Centre) A Great Horned Owl with its prize of a gray squirrel. The rarely seen Lap Owl (bottom) moments before an attack.

57

ments, they are not generally a threat to domestic fowl. They are, however, vital links in the food chain of the deep woodland, lowland forest, and swamp, and as such should not be killed.

The owl that probably established the family as a portent of doom is the Eastern Screech Owl (*Otus asio*). In spite of its name, this bird wails and moans dolefully, but rarely screeches. In fact, the great horned owl can produce a much more terrifying scream. Because they are so silent in their flight and furtive in their behavior, it is the more surprising when an owl emits a hair-raising scream. It can then look stern and dignified, as if it could not possibly have been responsible for such a sound. No wonder these predators have traditionally been the mystical mascots of magicians and astrologers.

The eastern screech owl is smaller than the great horned owl. Its wing-spread is 18 to 24 inches, and its body length is only 6½ to 10 inches. Unlike other birds of prey, it prefers 'town-dwelling' and roosts in the trees of suburbs, small villages and farms. It may build its simple nest of sticks, vegetation and feathers in deserted buildings or in woodpecker holes in trees.

This owl is a good example of the natural assistance this group of birds offers man. Screech owls search for mice and other rodents among hay-stacks, eating all types of crop-damaging rodents and insects. They also include some frogs, snakes, worms, and nestlings in their diet. The Barn Owl (*Tyto alba*) helps the farmer by eating katydids, grasshoppers, mice, rats, starlings, and sparrows.

The Long-eared Owl (*Asio otus*) is named for its conspicuous ear tufts, an unusual feature among birds. It is a most graceful species. It inhabits coniferous forests.

Another inhabitant of deep forest solitude is *Strix varia* (Northern Barred Owl), which has a smoothly rounded head and no ear tufts. Although seldom seen, this bird of prey is very numerous, and its loud mating hoots are often heard for miles. *Strix* has a varied vocal repertoire, including croaks, cackles, gibbers, gobbles, and clucks, the scope of which its common

name, 'Eight-Hooter,' scarcely conveys.

Like other owls, *Strix* is a capable hunter of small mammals, birds, and insects. It will occasionally take another owl, pigeon, chicken, grouse, bobwhite, or jay. Crows and jays sometimes mob the sleeping owl and drive the bewildered creature from its roost. How do certain birds know that they may bedevil their natural enemies, with minimal risk, during the day? What is beneficial about mobbing behavior? Derek MacDonald, J. D. Goodwin and Helmut Adler said that the jays and crows are practicing defense behaviors in what appears to be a play routine. Mobbing may also discharge 'nervousness' and thus embolden the group, strengthening its protective reflexes and decreasing the chances of ineffectual panic.

Hawks

The birds of prey that dive for goslings are most often some species of hawks and falcons of the families Accipitridae and Falconidae. The 55 species contained in these families have thickly-feathered heads, sharp, curved beaks, and strong talons at the ends of knobby toes. Unlike the owls, who kill at night by stealth, the hawks and falcons kill by day with great speed and agility.

The Eastern Goshawk (*Accipiter gentilis*) is anything but gentle. It strikes swiftly, impetuously, but with complete control, taking domestic poultry, rabbits, rodents, and insects that come into view.

The other and more common poultry hawk is Cooper's Hawk (*Accipiter cooperii*). Game birds and poultry form more than one quarter of its diet, and it takes few insects or rodents. Cooper's Hawk is brave and will strike prey too heavy for it to carry away. When chased from a conquest the bold hawk may even show attack behavior before taking flight. The Cooper's Hawk normally inhabits forests, woodlands, and coniferous groves where it regulates birdlife balance, consuming a great variety of small birds.

Noel and Helen Snyder studied Cooper's Hawks nesting. Even this dauntless predator must have its enemies because the mother hawk was

*The Goshawk (*Accipiter gentilis*) can carry off mammals and birds the size of grouse.*

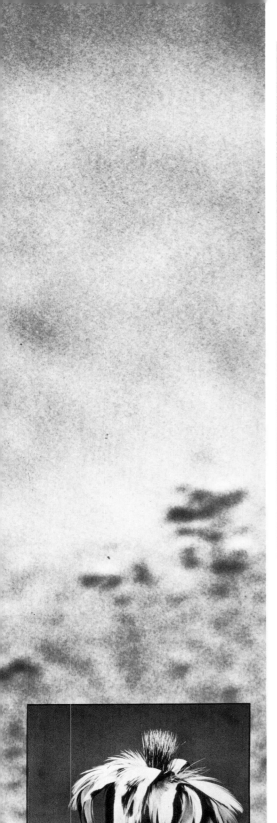

suddenly missing from her incubating eggs. Some of them were cracked, as if the female had been pounced upon from above, perhaps by a goshawk or great horned owl. All that remained were a few of her feathers at the foot of the tree that held the nest. Her monogamous mate, which had built most of the nest with sticks, bark, moss, and grass, tried to hatch the eggs himself, but without the naked area of skin on the breast, called a 'brood patch,' he could not keep them warm enough.

The father hawk was given other nestlings to foster, and he did a fair job, learning slowly to tear small pieces of chipmunk off, instead of presenting his empty beak. He also learned to hold his head high when feeding the young, who often mistook his red eye for a piece of meat. The naturalists had to keep the nestlings warm at night, how-

ever, because the father did not care to try brooding again. Between human and hawk efforts, the nestlings were finally fledged.

Trying to understand the local decline in numbers of goshawk and other species, human observers have examined eggshells and found that they contain DDE, a breakdown product of DDT, which is correlated to thinner shells and reduces the chances of embryos maturing. The mother hawk will generally desert a nest once these brittle shells crack. Because the hawks, especially in the eastern United States, eat many small birds that migrate from Mexico and Central America, where DDT is still heavily used, they incorporate the poisons in their systems. The species have become nearly extinct in the east because of the combined effects of DDT on shell integrity and nesting and mating behavior. The species is also threatened by humans shooting them or taming them for falconry.

The kestrel uses its long tail to hover over prey. It carries a catch off to a safe place to feed (far left and above). (Left) A Peregrine Falcon wearing a hood.

Eagles

Birds, in general, make very good parents. The big predatory birds are no exception. Even masterful eagles do not disdain the job. Seton Gordon and his wife observed the Golden Eagle (*Aquila chrysaëtos*) in Scotland, in 1927, at a time when fears of anthropomorphic attribution had not reached present neurotic proportions. Their patience and love for the birds produced a remarkable record of eagle parenthood in their book *Days with the Golden Eagle*.

An eagle eyrie is usually four to seven feet wide and three to five feet thick. It is used repeatedly by the same couple. A nest can be used for 30 to 50 years in succession by the breeding pair, which are apparently mated to each other for life.

From steep, heavily wooded mountain tops, the male and female adult eagles soar up above the clouds and stoop at great speed to their prey, which can be duck, grouse, wild turkey, or waterfowl, a racoon, rabbit, skunk, fox, or young deer. Crowned Eagles (*Stephanoaetus coronatus*) in Africa have even killed half-grown bushbuck by the power of their clutch alone. The creature is dismembered and hidden in different trees. In times of wild game scarcity, the golden eagle may seek domestic poultry, calves, and lambs.

It is not known precisely how eagles learn to hunt, but their early experiences in the nest prepare them for rugged exposure and competition.

In almost every case, eagles breed only two eggs, which inevitably hatch into one male and one female. Although the parents keep the eyrie well-stocked with food in the first six weeks of their offsprings' lives, the young do not get equal portions. For some reason the female, always born larger, is fed first and most. She is strong and very aggressively attacks her weak brother. Frequently, this results in the death of the male. The purpose of this sexual competition is still mysterious, but certainly the female 'repays' the species by hatching her many broods, and feeding and protecting her young during cold storms.

The hen eagle feeds the young eaglets bits of hare and eats the bones herself. She is assisted in hunting for the family by the cock, which brings game, like ptarmigan, squirrel, roe deer calf, weasel, fox cub, and jackdaw to the nest. The adult male may feed the eaglets also.

By six weeks of age the white down of the young eagles has been replaced by dark brown feathers. Even the legs are covered with feathers, so that the eagles look like they are wearing quilted trousers. The female will grow to be 35 to 41 inches from head to tail with a wingspread of up to 92 inches.

The Bald Eagle (far left) is the national symbol of the United States of America. It fishes around estuaries, and was once numerous in Florida. Sadly, its numbers are now depleted. Centre left is the vividly colored Bataleur Eagle, which is found in Southern Africa, and hunts small mammals like the African Hare (above). The Golden Eagle (left) lives in mountainous territory and flies for many miles, especially in winter, to find its prey. They hunt over areas of moorland where they can dive to catch prey.

The huntsmen of Kirgiziya, Soviet Central Asia, have used the Golden Eagle for centuries to hunt down foxes and wolves (below). This eagle will build its nest on exposed rock or cliff, and hunt over many square miles of moor away from the nest. It can stay on the wing for many hours, scanning the ground beneath for a catch such as the fox (right).

The mature male, however, is smaller, with a body length between 30 and 35 inches and wingspan of 84 inches.

At the time of first feathering, the eaglets begin stretching and exercising their wings. As summer progresses, they feed themselves off the carcasses supplied by their parents. But gradually the parents decrease the food supply, and the nest becomes less comfortable because of the hatching of summer flies. At about nine weeks of age, the young eagles test their wings and return after flight to the nest for the remaining food. After another week, they go off with the adults, presumably learning to fly and hunt well from the experts, and then they move off to new territory.

There are 80 species of eagles throughout the world. Sadly, some are near extinction in certain places. For example, more than 100,000 Southern Bald Eagles (*Halieatus leucocephalus*) have been shot in Alaska, since a bounty of 50c per bird was established. This species is the national emblem of the United States. Like so many other species toward which man is ambivalent, the eagle is revered and hunted. Legends say that the eagle rejuvenates itself by gazing straight at the sun or by plunging into the sea. But the eagle is no more immortal than other endangered species of snakes, sharks, and tortoises. The image of the eagle was cast on tablets and royal seals in 4,000 B.C. It was the first bird of prey to be represented graphically, and its wings, that may spread to nine or ten feet, span the centuries majestically. Human population growth and the consequent extension of civilization have, however, reduced the natural habitat of eagles, and soon their outline on ancient coins, banners, and military standards may be all that remains of this beautiful bird.

No predatory bird should be molested in its natural habitat. In the wild, they regulate the wild bird population. On farms and near other human settlements, they minimize damage by rodent and insect pests. Apart from this, it would seem that creatures which can spot a one-inch, green grasshopper across 100 yards of meadow, or can stay on the wing for eight hours, covering 300 miles a day, deserve respect and preservation.

Defense against birds of prey

The defense patterns of small predatory birds, which are prey of large raptorial birds, are a good example of how species interact. As mentioned before, the animals preyed upon are not weak and spiritless. Natural selection 'keeps' structures and behaviors which are well adapted for defense, and 'discards' maladapted ones. For instance, ground-dwelling species of birds would not survive long, if they had not the innate or learned ability to dart to cover and call in alarm the moment they notice an animal of prey. Their flocking together at the approach of a predator is protective because the hawk, falcon, or owl will rarely break into a dense group.

The grouse have two methods of defending themselves, each suited to a different predator. When a Peregrine Falcon (*Falco peregrinus*) is sighted they hang together on the ground, seeming to know that this enemy will catch them best in the air. When a Golden Eagle (*Aquila chryseatos*) swoops, however, the grouse fly up, again seeming to realize this enemy has greatest success snatching them from the ground. The Golden Eagle is strong enough to take grouse to its nest in a high cliff.

Experience and instinct combine, in as yet unknown proportions, to permit the recognition of predators. There are some recognition patterns that seem more genetically controlled than others. Goslings, for example, scatter under the approaching shadow of a goose. This seems to be very discriminating and purposive behavior for ones so young and simple of brain. A broad shadow produces a commotion, but if the goose approaches from a direction which causes a narrow shadow, it produces no reaction.

The explanation may lie in the eye-brain connections ordered by gosling genes, and not the result of gosling cleverness. When the broad shadow approaches, more cells on the retinas of the goslings' eyes are stimulated simultaneously. This stimulation may be directly communicated to parts of the brain which, when excited to a certain threshold, precipitate the escape behaviors. The approach of the narrow shadow stimulates only a few retina cells, insufficient to trigger the retreat pattern. This system is not foolproof because raptors sometimes approach at an angle which might not create a broad enough shadow to stimulate the necessary number of retina cells and the goslings can be caught.

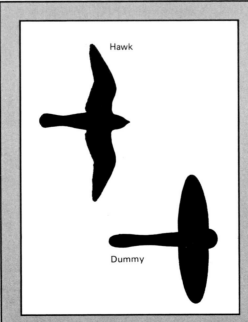

Living under a shadow
When a mother goose approaches her young in a way which makes a broad shadow, they flee in fright. The shadow, like the dummy (left), resembles a predatory hawk.

The shadow of the narrow end of the dummy (right) stimulates fewer of the goslings' retina cells. The shape is like the long neck of a flying goose and does not cause the goslings to react.

PART FOUR

THE PREDATORS ON LAND

The stalk and pounce,
the chase and kill . . .
and the escape from man

Many amphibians, reptiles and mammals occupy the land. Thus they move over land and make their living upon the land. Seals, which are mammals, certain fishes, crocodiles, and marine turtles, which are reptiles, come to land for short periods. They bask in the sun, or munch on insects, or deposit their eggs. But none of these are land animals because they do not spend most of their time or find most of their food on land.

Of the three classes of vertebrates – amphibians, reptiles, mammals – with species presently occupying land, mammals are the most recently evolved and the most dominant.

(Previous page) The Tiger yawns and shows the teeth it uses to tear the flesh of prey.

Amphibians

Amphibians were dominant on land 350 million years ago. They had evolved from air-breathing fishes, which had developed the ability to move about on land, like the modern Australian Mudskipper (*Periopthalmus koelreuteri*).

Amphibians moved on land but also were bound to water for reproduction. Even today, amphibians lead a double existence, moving freely over land but periodically returning to water to moisten their skin and lay eggs.

There are now about 2,100 species of amphibians, including the familiar salamanders, newts, frogs, and toads.

Of these species, several are carnivorous, and their diets consist mainly of insects. Only the Brazilian Horned Toad (*Ceratophrys dorsata*) makes a steady diet of vertebrate prey, swallowing up other frogs in its huge mouth. Amphibians are small predators and often have the tables turned on them, when they themselves are seized as prey by reptiles, birds, or mammals.

In their predatory habits, frogs and toads (Order: Anura, of the Class: Amphibia) are often remarkable for their large appetites and curious feeding adaptations. For instance, the frog (*Bufo americanus*) may eat 22,700

(Below) The Giant American Bullfrog has its natural habitat in North America. It is one of the largest members of the frog family.

Mexican Bean Beetles in the period from May to September, and the toad (*Rhinophrynus*) burrows with its shovel-shaped first toe to find termite tidbits underground.

Evidently, amphibians can provide some members of the animal world with some relief from a potentially smothering blanket of insects. Unfortunately, some of the little anuran insect traps are too efficient for their own good, as they snap up every moving thing of the proper dimensions. For example frogs (*Bufo bufo* and *Bufo marimus*) may flick their long tongues at and swallow a bee or the poisonous petals of a Strychnine Tree. Sometimes the individual can learn to suppress the snapping reflex; sometimes the reflex is irresistible.

That fatalities result from the inborn urges of predators is frequently overlooked. Eating savagely, quickly, mechanically has its risks. A predator may choke on its meal, as the pike-eating pike (*Esox lucius*) has. A predator may be poisoned by its prey, like the hawk *Stephanoaëtus* attempting to eat a poisonous snake, or slowed down by a huge meal, as *Python sebae* after eating a buck, only to become easy prey itself. Even a skilled carnivorous cat, like the leopard (*Panthera pardus*) may be injured or killed by the fatal slash of warthog tusks during a life and death struggle.

(Below) A common frog deals a deadly blow to the worm. Crested newts (right) return to water to lay their eggs on water plants.

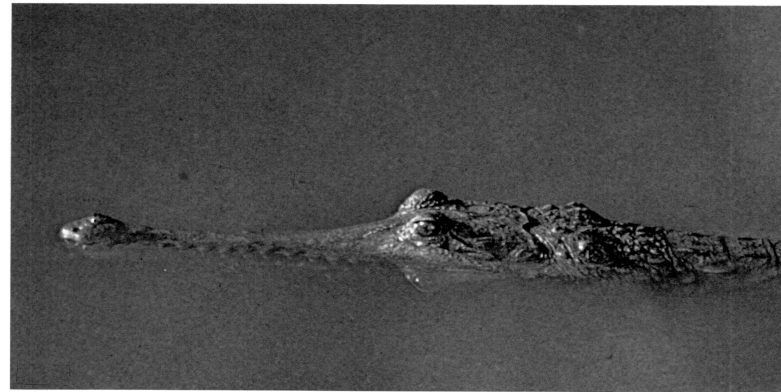

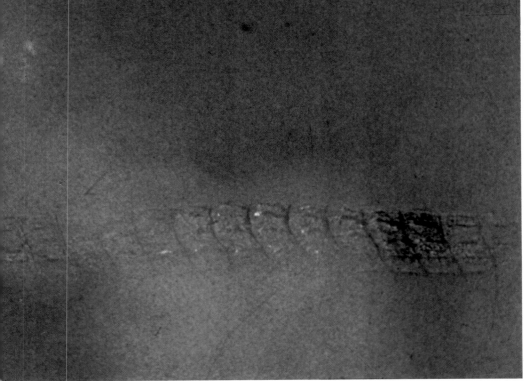

Reptiles

Species of reptiles that had evolved from amphibian ancestors, began to multiply and displace amphibians on the land 270 million years ago. The great biological advantage that reptiles had over amphibians was their ability to lay and hatch eggs on land. In addition, locomotion on land was perfected and the ability to maintain skin condition without immersion in water was improved. In the time since then, many reptiles evolved further and returned to water, like certain turtles, snakes, and crocodiles. There are approximately 6,000 species of reptiles that now exist in all ecozones, and most are predatory. The land reptiles fall into three groups, turtles, lizards, snakes.

Top left is a gharial. The Crocodylidae family has three members: true crocodiles, alligators and caymans. Centre left, the Saltwater Crocodile. Below left, Johnston's Crocodile. Above, Alligators bask by an Indian lake.

Turtles

Most turtles are herbivorous, but some species of the Testunidae family are carnivorous. The Galápagos Turtle (*Testudo*), which eats insects, molluscs and worms, was observed to catch and eat two rats and a pigeon while in captivity. It would even eat raw meat greedily.

The fact that predators can modify their diets when food availability changes is important to note. Except in cases of extreme specialization of the teeth, sensory organs and/or digestive system for just one type of food, all vertebrates have a margin of dietary flexibility. If changes in a species' diet become permanent, behavioral and structural changes in the organism may follow, consistent with the advantages they provide in acquiring and assimilating the new food.

Lizards

Most lizards are insectivorous, but some species feed on other lizards, small birds and eggs. The large Monitor Lizard (*Varanus gouldi*) can even down a pig or deer.

The Tokay lizards of the Dutch East Indies and Philippines are unusual for the Gekkonidae family. They may be more than one foot long (one third of which is tail), and have extremely powerful jaws. Their relatives, the pygopodid lizards of Australia are even more distinctive with snakelike bodies that can be almost a yard long. Again, most of the body is tail, and this can be shed and regrown after an enemy's attack. These lizards are nocturnal and fossorial (burrowing underground), and they eat smaller lizards.

The subtle chameleons are largely insect-eaters. They live in trees, and some of the larger of the 80 extant species can eat small birds.

In the families of lizards called Heladermatidae and Varanidae, there are three notable species of predators, which are The Gila Monster (*Heloderma suspectum*), the Mexican Beaded Lizard (*Heloderma horridum*), and the Monitor Lizard (*Varanus gouldi*). As their names imply, these are formidable creatures. Some are as large as

(Left) A Snapping Turtle exercises its very strong jaw. (Above) A young Green Turtle, a species found around the shores of Queensland. (Below) A tree-climbing Monitor Lizard.

crocodiles, which are not members of the lizard suborder, Lacertilia.

Heloderma are natives of the south-western United States. They prey upon nestling mammals. Their venom, which drains from glands in the lower jaw onto 2·5 inch-long teeth, seems more important in defense than in feeding.

Provoked Gila Monsters will bite people, and their venom can cause many symptoms, such as nausea, sweating, sore throat, ringing in the ears, faintness, or collapse.

The Monitor Lizard is found in the East Indies, Africa, and Australia. Although primarily terrestrial (on land), it will swim and even climb trees in pursuit of small mammals.

The chameleon (above and left) uses its long tongue to capture prey. The tuatara (below) usually preys on insects, but will occasionally take birds.

Snakes

Snakes are the principal reptilian land predators today. There are about 2,700 species of Serpents, as the order is called, and these are divided into several families. Four of these families, Boidae, Colubridae, Elapidae, and Viperidae, contain predatory species of which some are giant constrictors, and some are poisonous.

Since predatory snakes have been much feared and mythologized, their natural histories, habits, and economic significance are interesting.

Boidae include the boa constrictor, anaconda, and pythons, which are all giants. Colubridae include many poisonous types, which use their venom to subdue their prey. One of these is the helpful King Snake (*Lamproeltis*), which will protect human communities by eating poisonous snakes.

The Elapidae are all species of cobras, corals, mambas, and kraits, while the Viperidae are all types of deadly vipers, adders, rattlesnakes, and bushmasters.

These families encompass great diversity of form and function. They range from less than two feet to more than 30, and their diets include everything from termites to young antelope and goats. Some species are aquatic, some terrestrial and arboreal, while others are subterranean.

Snakes have very varied reproductive systems. They may give birth to live young that mature in the oviducts, and feed off the egg yolk, whilst still inside the mother, or they may lay eggs that mature externally, sometimes with the protection of the mother, sometimes alone. Occasionally, it appears that the female has the choice of retain-

ing or laying the eggs. She holds back the young for internal development if a warm safe place for egg deposition is unavailable. In some species, the rudiments of a placenta are found.

Smaller species of snakes may live for up to ten years, while larger ones can live for more than twenty. Even when decapitated, a venomous snake is potentially dangerous. The head is still 'alive' and may even strike and discharge its poison. The body may squirm for up to seven hours after decapitation, and the heart may continue beating for more than a day. These

facts plus the astonishing strength of some species, the skin-shedding habit, the ability to fast, for more than two years in some cases, and hibernate for long periods underground, followed by an apparent return to life, have all combined to conjure the image of the immortal snake in the folklore of many communities. Folklore also gave rise to the name of the family of snakes, the Boidae. In the Middle Ages, people thought certain snakes wrapped themselves around cows' udders and drank their milk. These snakes were named 'boas' from the Italian word *bove*,

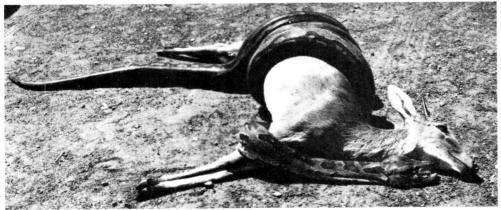

(Top) A Florida Four-lined Chicken Snake catches and consumes its normal prey. The snake kills the chicken by trapping it by the neck in its jaws. The jawbones of the snake can be unhinged to allow the passage of large masses of food. (Above left) The Boa Constrictor kills its prey, which is usually small mammals, by coiling itself around the animal and squeezing it to death. (Above) An African snake swallowing a toad whole. The unhinged jaw can be seen quite clearly. (Far left) A farmer near Bulawayo, Southern Rhodesia, could not understand why calves occasionally disappeared. The mystery was soon solved when he discovered this bloated python sleeping off its meal in a bush. (Left) The cries of the duiker attracted a farmer who shot the attacking python.

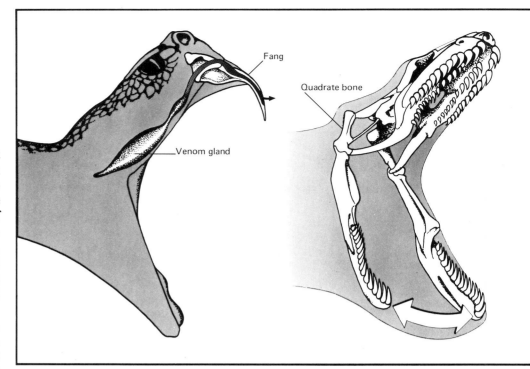

meaning ox. But in spite of a great flexibility in the prey preferences shown by these snakes, milk does not seem to be on the menu. The 'boids' include many small sand-burrowing types of the genus *Eryx*, as well as the giant constrictors of the genera *Boa*, *Epicrates*, *Eunectes*, and *Python*. Pythons are Old World species, while the other genera have species in both the New and Old Worlds.

The burrowing boas live in sandy, stony places all across North America, the Middle East, and Eastern Europe down to India and Ceylon. They are short, as snakes go, being about three feet in length. They strike small rodents, lizards, and birds when these move the sand. Their young are born live in litters of 18 to 20, each baby being about five inches long. These sand boas are less impressive than their constrictor cousins when they go in pursuit of food, or in defense. Defense is accomplished by the snake rolling itself into a tight ball.

Boa constrictors are heavy, muscled types that may grow exceptionally to 20 feet. Normally, a boa is full grown at 10 to 12 feet and is sufficiently strong to overpower a man. This occurs rarely and almost always only at man's instigation. They prefer to coil around lizards, birds, mongooses, rats, and squirrels. Snakes generally shy away from man, just as most men shy away from them. Boids are not poisonous. They inhabit mild desert, tropical rainforest, and fields of sugar cane. They can be found at sea level and at all altitudes up to 2,000–3,000 feet.

One of the species (*Eunectes murines*), or anaconda as it is commonly known, is aquatic, inhabiting the rivers of South America. It is the giant of all snake giants, with a record length presently set at 37·5 feet.

With increasing length and weight these snakes have sacrificed their speed and agility. Although they have few enemies, they have retained the hiss warning used by smaller species to discourage predators. Hissing is produced by the forced explusion of air from the left lung (the right one being much smaller) and a special reservoir sac at the end of the lung. Hissing or rattling sounds may act like conditioned stimuli. As they come to be associated in the mind of the prey animal with the

dangerous strike of the snake, they elicit the desired response, and the prey avoids the snake.

While killing their prey by constriction, the great snakes run the risk of being injured by their quarry. This happened when a python tried to overpower the leading male of a troop of baboons. With his long, powerful canines the baboon tore a chunk of flesh out of the python. Assisted by the cheers and darting assaults of other troop members, the baboon finally went free, and the injured snake died. Such an incident is unusual because pythons like other predators will select easy prey. Boas very sensibly avoid big baboons, sharp-tusked warthogs and wild pigs. They prefer their quarry young and docile, such as rabbits, hens, and ducks, and, if they can get them, baby ocelots and even dogs. While swallowing a meal whole, the mouth is so distended that the snake can not breathe for several minutes at a time. It must stop the swallowing process and push its sturdy trachea forward to permit inhalation. A very large meal can take hours to swallow and months to digest. A naturalist, R. M. Isemonger, once saw an African Rock Python (*Python sebae*), which grows to 15 feet, single out for attack a yearling from a family of bushbuck drinking at a water hole. After sinking its curved fangs into the neck of the victim, the python then wrapped its coils around the buck's body and squeezed until suffocation was complete. Like all snakes, the python quickly investigated the carcass with its tongue, before deciding to

(Left) The hawk's failure to catch the Boomslang Snake at first strike was fatal. The snake had time to give it a venomous bite. (Above) An Indian snake charmer.

swallow it head first. The buck was eaten in 38 minutes, and the python withdrew to a rock shelter for a two week rest. When next seen, the python was somewhat slimmer, but the digestive juices had not yet decomposed the body much, and the snake would probably have been satisfied for months to come had not the naturalist dissected it to examine the stomach contents.

Little is known about the reproductive aspect of boid life. Like other types of snakes, they mate infrequently, perhaps once a year. The courtship may take up to two hours, during which time the male uses his vestigial hindlimbs or 'spurs' to scratch and coax the female to arch her cloacal opening toward him. Observations of copulation are sparse, but observations of snake penises are numerous and detailed due to the fact that they were used as criteria for species classification. Snake penises are usually paired and very elaborate in design, with spines, barbs, and in the case of large boas many fleshy folds. This complexity of structure, which is hidden most of the time because the organ is withdrawn into the base of the tail when unused, may insure the success of union. Copulation without the assistance of limbs is difficult, especially since the position must be maintained for one hour or longer. After this the female is left swollen, presumably with a generous supply of sperm. Snake sperm can stay viable in the female for months and even years. Therefore it is hard to accurately determine the period of internal development before deposition of eggs or birth of the young.

Large boas, like the small sand-burrowing types, give birth to live

young. There are 21 to 64 in a litter, and each snakelet is about 20 inches long. Pythons, in contrast, lay 20 to 50 eggs at a time, and in some species the mothers brood their pile of eggs for as long as a month without interruption. Eggs must be kept warm (about 90 degrees Fahrenheit), for proper development. Snake females generally try to provide a source of warmth, either by laying their eggs on decomposing vegetation, which gives off heat as it rots, or by exposing the eggs to sunlight, or both.

Those species that incubate the eggs show some ability to maintain a body temperature higher than the environmental temperature. It is very unusual for a cold-blooded animal, like a fish, amphibian, or snake, to be able to raise its body temperature higher than that of its surroundings for a prolonged period of time. Some of the brooding snakes seem to be able to accomplish this by continuous muscular quivering.

The Colubrid snake family contains the only species of snake observed to make a rough nest, and this is the King Cobra (*Ophiaphagus hannah*). The female piles up sand and bamboo slivers into a nest about 18 inches high and 36 inches wide. She brings leaves to the spot by looping the front half of her body around them, and she hollows out the inside by moving round and round in circles, smoothing the inside of the nest. After two days of work, she lays her eggs, covers them with sticks and leaves, then coils herself on top of them.

King Cobras also hold the distinction of being the world's longest, poisonous snakes. An exceptional individual measured 18 feet but, generally, they are about eight feet. They grow rapidly in the first year of life, from about 12 inches to three or four feet. Thereafter, they grow at ever slower rates. Reptiles, amphibians, and fishes all grow continuously through life. Unlike mammals and birds, which have an accelerated and discrete growing period, poikilotherms (cold-blooded species) never stop growing.

Reptiles and amphibians also have different degrees of ability to regrow certain injured or amputated parts of their bodies. This power of regeneration is very much reduced in mammals and in birds.

Besides regeneration, cobras have many other defenses in form and action. Many of them spread their anterior ribs into the characteristic threatening hood. Others play dead by half rolling over and dropping their jaws. When some animal comes over to investigate, the snake sprays or spits venom straight into the eyes of the inquisitive one.

Knowing that cobras are all deadly poisonous, it is remarkable that Burmese charmers dare to kiss the snake on the head, at the climax of a shrine ceremony. If the venom entered their blood, the charmers could die within a short time. However, with cobra poisoning there would be an accompanying sense of indifference that makes the death less unpleasant. This may be why Cleopatra probably chose the Egyptian Cobra to effect her suicide. Bernhard Grzimek reports that the striking speed of poisonous snakes is slower than most people imagine. Rattlesnakes strike at 8·5 feet per second, and cobras at about 1·5 feet per second. A skilled charmer can pat a cobra on the head, while it is striking.

Snake poisons are neurotoxins. This means they interfere with the proper function of the nerves, particularly those that carry messages to the muscles. The krait, another colubrid snake, has venom that competes with the neurotransmitter (a chemical that permits passage of impulses from one nerve to another or to a muscle), acetylcholine. Since the toxin blocks the path of acetylcholine, messages can not be delivered from nerves to muscles and paralysis results. The muscles become limp and the victim cannot direct them to move.

Snakes are generally immune to their own venom, and certain of their mammalian predators have evolved a degree of immunity also. The mongoose, meerkat, and cangamba (a type of skunk), which try to eat snakes, avoid death through this immunity and by fast dodging movements that evade the fangs.

As far as human immunity to poisonous bites goes, there is little evidence for any inherent resistance except for the alleged immunity of the Psylli people of North Africa. These people have helped rid houses, gardens, and fields of snakes for centuries. It is their hereditary profession and their supposed genetic resistance to bites that has cast them in this peculiar role for a long time. The Psylli seem to exude an odor that repels the snakes, and certain intermittent changes occur in their behavior and body chemistry when they deal with snakes. There is evidence (Pliny, 1500 B.C.) that the Psylli were extremely bizarre. They tested the legitimacy of questionable infants by exposing them to poisonous snakes, which was probably a very effective form of endogenous selection for the repelling ability. Whether or not an offspring had the supposed biochemical trait, it probably was too young to bring it out through the excited tension and frenzy that adults show during charming and chanting. Hence, some infants with the trait were lost, but since all who were tested and did not have the trait were sacrificed also, there was a genetic benefit in terms of perpetuated immunity.

The Psylli, who originally derived their anti-snake power from a word given them by Ra, the Egyptian Sun God, became Moslems, in the 12th century conversions in North Africa. As travelling dervishes and mendicants, they would entertain caravans departing for Mecca by dancing with snakes. Their faces were contorted like the insane, and, foaming at the mouth, they would sometimes bite the snakes.

Travellers thought that touching a Psylli in such a trance was good protection against a snake attack on the journey.

Many people who are bitten do survive, if the skin is just scratched and little poison enters the blood. Early administration of antivenom, the snake poison antidote, saves them, but they usually suffer the general effects of the bite – drooping eyelids, difficulty swallowing, giddiness, weakness, gasping, and in the case of rattlesnakes (*Crotalus*), the 'broken neck effect,' in which the muscles lose all tone and the neck can break from lack of support before the antivenom takes effect.

Fortunately, the antidote reverses the effect of cobra bites completely. Often, the only lasting effect of an attack is the discoloration, atrophy or amputation of the bitten part, if gangrene occurs as the result of tourniquet or infection. Luckily snakes have evolved many warning signals to discourage accidental trampling or attack by their own predators. Signals like hissing, rattling, and strong cloacal odors sometimes have spared human beings the consequences of an instinctive defensive or predatory strike by a snake.

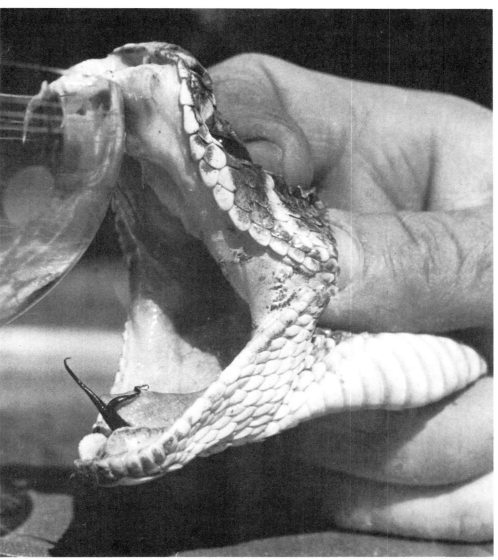

The African Cobra above has risen to the attack and spread its shield. (Right) The venom from the fangs of a Diamondback Rattlesnake being milked into a glass.

81

Mammals on land

Probably due to the fact that we are mammals, and that many of the predatory mammals are gregarious like us, many more detailed observations of these types are available than of other land predators.

Mammals are the dominant land animals today, and they began their history as land masters 65 million years ago, when they first started to displace reptiles, from which they had originated 35 million years earlier.

The 3,200 species of living mammals are divided into 16 orders, mostly comprised of plant-eating species. The orders Lagomorpha (hares), Ungulates (hooved animals), and Subungulates (elephants) are non-predatory. The Orders Chiroptera (bats), Rodentia (rodents), and Primates (monkeys, apes, and man) contain a few predatory species, but most are herbivorous. Only the orders Marsupalia (pouched mammals), Carnivora (meat-eaters), Insectivora (insect-eaters), Cetacea (whales and dolphins), and Pinnipedia (semi-marine mammals, like walruses) contain important mammalian predators. Of these, Carnivora contains the largest mammalian land predators.

Marsupalia
There are a few interesting but nearly extinct predators in this order. The marsupial 'cat' (*Dasyurus viverrinus*), and the Tasmanian 'wolf' (*Thylacinus cynocephalus*) and 'devil' (*Sarcophilus harrisii*) are all pouched mammals. They are inhabitants of Australia, New Guinea, Tasmania, and Aru Islands.

The 'cat' is small, spotted, and weighs no more than three kilograms. It is agile on the ground and in trees, feeding on insects and small vertebrates.

The 'wolf' species have strong canine teeth. They look like dogs and can eat large wallabies. The other large pouched Tasmanian carnivore is the 'devil' which weighs up to ten kilograms and feeds on small vertebrates.

The 'devil' is a very robust creature, and can weigh up to 20 pounds. It is nocturnal, and builds its nest in the forest and bush of Tasmania. The devil feeds generally on small mammals, and by scavenging.

Rodentia

Rodents occupy land, semi-aquatic, arboreal, and subterranean habitats. There are more species of Rodentia than in any other mammalian order. Most of these species provide the bulk of prey for reptilian, avian, and mammalian predators. In spite of the fact

A Tasmanian devil (left) hunting at night in its natural habitat of underbrush and forest. A common shrew (above) tackles an earthworm. The shrew is found all over the world except in Australia and polar regions and is a voracious insect-eater.

that most rodents are strict vegetarians, some species also eat insects, fish, birds, and birds' eggs. For instance, doormice can eat eggs and nestlings, as well as their other favorite tree foods of fruit, nuts, and insects.

Another historically interesting property of these little mammals is that they can lose and regenerate their tails, like lizards. This unusual ability among the mammals, the retention of such a primitive feature, emphasizes their reptilian origin.

Carnivora

The carnivores are placental mammals which have existed in their present form for only the past two million years. They have developed in pace with the herbivorous mammals, especially hooved herds, on which they prey. Their evolutionary history has been affected greatly by man, who is a competing predator, a hunter of carnivores, and recently, but too late in many cases, a friend and protector. In some instances man has reversed the damage.

Cheetah

The beautiful cheetah (Hindi word meaning spotted one) was once plentiful throughout much of Africa, Arabia, Persia, India, and Russian Turkestan. Now it is extinct in India and rare in Pakistan, Afghanistan, and southwestern Africa. Cheetahs are sighted most frequently in open grassland, where they climb trees or elevated places for a lookout. They also live in more arid or more densely wooded areas, depending on the prey available.

Cheetahs are in the same family (Felidae) with *Panthera* cats, the lions, leopards, and tigers, but they are placed in a different genus because they followed a separate evolutionary course and have become somewhat distinct in form and behavior from the other cats.

They are the smallest carnivorous felids that roam the Serengeti Plain and they are built for speed rather than power. They purr like housecats, and although they sometimes growl and

snarl at other big cats, in order to convince them in their own language not to poach on cheetah kills, they cannot roar.

A fully grown cheetah measures six to eight feet from the nose to the tip of the tail and weighs 110 to 140 pounds. The face and head seem small compared to the long back and robust hindquarters. Nevertheless, they have elegant postures. They hold their heads erect, giving a haughty impression rather than a languid, lounging effect,

typical of lions. Their golden eyes are dark-rimmed, and a black line runs straight down from the inner corner of the eye to the outer edge of the mouth. This is the tear line, and it may be of adaptive value in several ways. Firstly, it may help the cheetah distinguish members of its own species from the leopard which is also spotted. It may disrupt the gaze of the prey, so that they do not become fixated in a staring contest with the cheetah, which normally will not attack an animal that

holds its ground. The tear line also emphasizes the mouth in certain threat gestures.

Coat and facial markings on animals are not simply ornamental. They usually protect the bearer from attack. For example, the black patches on the back surfaces of cheetahs' ears may deceive predators which approach from behind, into thinking they are a pair of alert eyes. This would be most help-

Cheetahs may purr like a housecat but they kill with great speed and dexterity.

ful to cheetahs at kill sites where they are more likely to be attacked by lions, leopards, and hyenas.

The skeleton and soft tissues of the cheetah have been hewn by natural selection to the demands of its existence. Apart from the long hindlimbs that provide great mechanical advantage in running and springing at prey, cheetahs have large nasal passages, bronchi, and lungs. The heart is large also, and the arteries have thick, muscular walls. All of these, plus large adrenal glands that produce mobilizing hormones, permit heavy breathing and sustained rapid heart beat and blood flow during the chase, which may exceed 70 miles per hour over 200 yards.

Natural selection has modified physiological function as well as form to complete the cheetah's adaptive interaction with its environment. The birth cycle, for example, is coordinated with the spring rainy season, before the vegetation has turned very green. This means the coat color of the cubs blends well with the dry, tan-colored grass and camouflages them while the mother is away hunting.

From about six to 12 months of age, cubs follow their mother's white-tipped tail through the tall grass. They observe her and learn to hunt. By 12 to 16 months, the cubs are effective predators. This first year of life is the most dangerous for cheetahs, and about half of all litters is lost through disease or attacks by other predators. Perhaps this is why cheetahs are able to reproduce rapidly, in 13 to 15 month intervals, which is faster than mountain lions, cougars, and other big cats.

Having escaped early death through injury or disease, a cheetah may live 15 to 20 years. This is rare in the wild. In order to protect this endangered species, scientists have sought to understand their interaction with prey populations more precisely.

Lions, leopards, cheetahs, hyenas, and wild hunting dogs are important in limiting the numbers of certain species of hooved herbivores in Nairobi Park and elsewhere. It is difficult to say, however, what impact they have on herd numbers compared to the impact that changes in habitat have on

Two cheetahs, one with a kill. The short grassland is typical of their territory.

the same herds. Randall Eaton (1974) and George Schaller (1972) made extensive field studies that show the food habits of the cheetah and other predators, with the object of providing information to help man maintain a balanced ecosystem in reserve areas.

Cheetahs seem best adapted to hunt swift antelope, but their diet has been shown to include smaller game, like baby warthogs and even hares. A large portion of cheetah kills in East Africa is made up of impala, Grant's and Thompson's Gazelles. Zebra, wildebeest, kongoni, and waterbuck are taken less frequently. The average weight of animals killed by cheetahs is 113 pounds. The predator finds it easier and safer to kill animals smaller and lighter than itself.

Different populations of cheetahs and different generations of the same population do take up distinct dietary preferences. Sometimes this is due to changing prey concentrations, and sometimes it is determined by the age, size, and sex composition of the predator group.

Although cheetahs are efficient hunters, there are some species that they pursue with infrequent success. It has been observed that cheetahs hunt ten species of prey, but they are rarely able to catch a single zebra, ostrich, or wildebeest. However, field records often rely on carcass location and identification of the predator by marks left on the corpse and tracks in the area, and it is sometimes possible to credit a kill to the wrong species or overlook small game kills that were consumed completely.

There are contradictory reports about the hunting methods of cheetahs. This is probably because the method is so variable. In Serengeti, cheetahs have been observed to hunt alone in 'open pursuit' rather than 'stalk and pounce.' Because cheetahs can sustain high speed running longer than other predators, they can afford the open pursuit approach. However, this technique will be modified according to the terrain and the size of prey. When neces-

Cheetahs will climb trees to watch for prey. They are built for speed and, once sighted, a prey has little chance of escape. The parents and cubs (far right) quickly tear apart the kill and devour it. If they delay, some other predator, such as a lion or tiger, could rob them of the meal which they have fought to obtain.

sary, cheetahs will slink from cover to cover and crouch like leopards before the final ambush. Such is the case when cheetahs stalk impala in the wooded savanna of Kruger Park. In Serengeti, where Thompson's Gazelle are the common prey and the tall grass provides good cover, the cheetah walks openly to its quarry, then rushes a gap of 150 to 200 metres at high speed. If cover is sparse, adults and even cubs will crawl close to the ground in pursuit of food. It is possible that stalking behavior is part of an inborn range of responses, as it is observed in cubs which have never had an adult model. When fully grown the cheetah can modify and omit parts of this range, including stalking.

Flexibility in hunting behavior extends to the degree of cooperation between cheetah adults on a hunt. Generally, cheetahs, like other felids, are solitary, but sometimes they have been seen hunting in pairs, when larger game, like wildebeest, is to be taken. The only truly social hunters are the lions (*Panthera leo*) which surround their prey in ambush.

In spite of their behavioral and anatomical specializations for hunting and in spite of their tendency to select older, weaker, or younger prey, cheetahs can kill only about once in every five attempts. They are often detected and sometimes attacked or outwitted by their prey. The kongoni and warthog, for instance, will slash and gore the cheetah with their pointed horns, especially when they are defending their young. Wild boar and adult Grant's Gazelle have reversed the order and killed cheetahs.

Indian tigers (*Panthera tigris*), in contrast to cheetahs, take many more types of game, including cattle and other domestic animals. At risk of disembowelment, tigers will even charge wild boar. One recorded success occurred when a tiger jumped on the back of its boar victim, thus avoiding its sharp tusks. These animals hunt at night, while cheetahs hunt in twilight, and bright moonlight. Tigers must get closer to their fleet prey than cheetahs, and they are often noticed before they can attempt the final rush. Neither tigers nor cheetahs waste energy on attacking alerted prey. Successful pounces usually occur from behind or

The leopard (above), the lion (right and below) and the tiger (far right) have teeth designed for holding and tearing their prey. Once their fangs have sunk into the neck or soft flanks of the pursued animal, the chase is over, and it is only time before the animal falls from exhaustion and lack of blood. Prey is carried off and the flesh is consumed quickly. The carcass is torn into pieces and gulped rapidly so that no other predator can steal the meal.

beside the victim, with puncture wounds being delivered quickly to the base of the skull and back of the neck. Simultaneously the head is twisted by the strong forepaws in an attempt to snap the vertebral column.

Hunting behavior is learned by all cats from the mother. Cheetahs, which are born in litters of three to six cubs, acquire the female's style of hunting and often her food preferences too. The mother uses vocal signals to direct her offspring. With one sound she bids very young cubs to wait in one spot while she hunts. With another sound she calls them to the kill. When the cubs begin to attend the hunt, they may spontaneously stalk and chase, but they are too inexperienced to tackle and grab the quarry. The mother may immobilize the victim for them, allowing them to learn to twist the head and sink their teeth into the ventral surface of the neck.

Since cheetahs are built for speed, they sacrifice the large heads, jaws, and teeth of other killers. While lions, leopards, and tigers can use canines to puncture the spine, and carnassial teeth behind the canines to crush bone, cheetahs cannot. Their teeth are not sturdy enough to crunch the cervical vertebrae. Therefore, they must learn

to strangle their victims and bite th soft under-surface of the neck, whi turning the prey's pointed horns t ward the ground. This gory perforn ance takes place without appare malice. No growling or display teeth precedes the attack. The runnir of the prey triggers the pursuit. Whe cheetahs catch up with the fleeir

theft because it is never followed by an attack.

Intraspecific (within a species) display is completely different from interspecific threat. Instead of growling, there is high-pitched yelping. Instead of lunging, there is direct swatting with the dew claw. Injuries are superficial, but the fur flies, and the clamor among several cheetahs which have been supplied with fresh meat in an experimental setting, looks and sounds more ferocious than it is. A submissive roll to the side or glance away is sufficient to thwart the confrontation.

In the wild, only a few cheetahs will attend a single kill. They know each other, respond to each other, according to pre-established positions in a stable hierarchy, and feed peaceably around one carcass. Furthermore, family groups of females with their young and adult hunting males have ways of minimizing overcompetition for food in one area. By marking spots along their paths of forage with scented urine, one group will turn another off its trail for at least 24 hours.

Odorous secretions are also used by estrus females to attract males. Thus scent-marking conveys important information about proximity and sexual availability to members of the same species. It is difficult for us, a visually- and auditory-oriented species, to appreciate the acuity of discrimination and the nuances of meaning in olfactory messages. Their significance is apparent throughout the world of mammalian predators.

prey, they sink their dew claw, which is a single, sharp claw on each forepaw, used in fighting and predation amongst members of the same species, into the animal's flank to bring the animal to the ground.

If a potential victim stands its ground, the cheetah may show that threat behavior which is used between species, consisting of growling, baring the teeth, and lunging. This display is likely to scare the animal into flight, triggering the chase. Interspecific threat gestures are also used by cheetahs when they try to defend prey from competing predators. They mimic the snarling, open mouth and growl display of other cats which come to steal their spoils. Unfortunately, this display is seldom effective in preventing the

Cheetahs hunt and move about in family groups. The territorial scent markings tell male cheetahs of the whereabouts of an estrus female. The period of gestation is three months, and the female usually has a litter of two to five cubs. Life in the wild is such, however, that only 50 per cent of cubs develop fully and survive into adulthood.

Spotted hyena

The spotted hyena also lives in the Serengeti Reserve. They are members of the order Carnivora, in their own family, Hyaenidae, which is related to the cats (Felidae), dogs (Canidae), and bears (Ursidae). They superficially resemble dogs and hunt very differently from their felid competitors. In many cases, hyenas are scavengers rather than predators.

Hyenas form 'clans' of up to 80 animals, which break into smaller groups when game is scarce. Groups of hyenas sometimes confront each other at scent-marked territorial borders, and they may even kill each other for border violations.

Like other predators of large animals, hyenas have dangerous anatomical equipment and aggressive instincts. Therefore, they have genetically programmed behavior mechanisms which help individuals of the same group to avoid destructive confrontations with one another.

There is surprisingly little physical difference between hyena males and females. There are even special adaptations of the external genetalia of females that make them look exactly like males. This lack of distinction is unusual in social, terrestrial mammals. In most of these species, males defend the group and are therefore larger and furnished with combative display features, like the mane of the male lion and the mantle and great canines of the male baboon. Among hyenas, however, males and females have approximately equal responsibilities in hunting and group defense. Therefore, they are about the same size, or females are slightly larger. Observers speculate that females dominate hyena society because of their role as guardians of the young. In addition to their size, females are, of course, distinguishable from the males when their udders are swollen with milk.

Hyenas are excellent hunters, both individually and in packs. Their sharp night vision, specialized teeth, strong necks and shoulders, and high speed running are just a few adaptations that

The hyena will not kill game if other food is available. The small elephant (right) might be a find rather than a kill. The vultures and Maribou Stalks (top right) feel quite secure in the presence of the hyena.

assist them. They mostly pursue wildebeest, zebra, and Thompson's Gazelle, adding an occasional buffalo, young rhinoceros, or warthog. Teamwork permits them to fell large and dangerous prey. Swift in the long run and in the wild, zigzag dash after small prey, a hyena can catch and swallow a hare in 55 seconds.

Although it may appear that predators have all the advantages, it is not true that prey species would thrive if predators were eliminated. Prey are acutely adapted to the behavior of their predators. The maintenance of these adaptations depends on the presence of the predator. If there were no predators, the prey would no longer perpetuate beautiful markings, fleet-running, pointed horns, or high strung alertness. They would decline as we know them.

Hyenas hunt in packs to bring down large prey like the wildebeest. The pack observes a herd of animals and singles out one. Hyenas have strong jaws and attack the prey's soft flanks.

Predators not only maintain the adaptive features of prey, but they also eliminate the maladaptive ones by killing weaker or diseased members of the herd. For example, a group of hyenas may scatter a herd of wildebeest, then stop and observe the animals to single out one for attack. What differences they can perceive are unknown, but eyewitness accounts of hyenas hunting relate that a selective process appears to be going on.

In Serengeti, hyenas take about twice as many male as female wildebeest. This may be the consequence of a high male-female wildebeest ratio or some peculiar attraction that male wildebeests hold for hyenas. Among zebra, more females are killed. Since female zebras come into estrus a few days after parturition, they are always pregnant. This means the sacrifice of an adult female zebra to hyenas is more damaging to the herd than the loss of a female from another prey group. Apart from

these cases, hyenas generally take equal numbers of both sexes of prey throughout their range in equatorial, east, and south Africa.

Hyenas will not kill any game if food is available for other reasons. They will eat animals which have died of disease, carcasses that belong to other predators, or refuse left by man. In this way they are economical with their energy and with life. On rare occasions this economy breaks down. In one incident alone 110 Thompson's Gazelle were killed in a single night. Only a few of the animals were eaten, some were left half-gnawed, others were untouched. It may be that on this dark, stormy night the plentiful gazelle did not signal to each other or run as they normally would have. It is also possible that the elements of the storm excited abnormally aggressive activity in the hyenas, just as an approaching thunderstorm excites violent dancing in a group of chimpanzees. But whether or

not a storm can induce overkill behavior in hyenas must remain speculation for now.

Even satiated hyenas can hunt and kill, just as satiated cheetahs eat a fresh carcass when it is presented to them in captivity. Perhaps this is an adaptation that counteracts seasonal prey scarcity. Sometimes a hyena will store surplus parts of kills in lakes or waterholes. Submerging the food in this way hides it from competing species. After some time, a hyena can return to its cache, stick its head under the muddy water, and drag out its snack of wildebeest or gazelle. This storage habit renders water undrinkable for humans in some areas.

Depending on the geography, type of game, competing predators, and proximity of human settlements, hyenas will divide their time in different proportions between hunting and scavenging. All Serengeti predators, except the aloof cheetah, will steal carrion when they can get their paws on it. Because hyenas wander over greater distances than the large predatory cats, they come across more carrion. In spite of this, it is probable that they eat their own kills 96% of the time. This contrasts sharply with the general belief that hyenas are exclusively scavengers. This idea might have arisen because hyenas eat carrion more often during

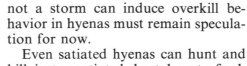

The spotted hyena has proportionately long limbs and large rounded ears. It makes a noise like laughter when it feeds.

the day, when people are awake and likely to see them, but they hunt and eat their own kills in the secrecy of darkness at night.

Whether eating their own or someone else's kill, hyenas are extremely well-adapted for total consumption of their prey, including meat, hide, bones, and hooves. They eat quickly. A single hyena can finish a baby Thompson's Gazelle in two minutes. A pack of 20 hyenas can eat a 100 kilogram yearling wildebeest in 13 minutes. Their conically shaped third premolars can crunch large bones, which they are perfectly capable of digesting. They excrete only the inorganic elements of the bone as a fine white powder. Upper fourth premolars shear against lower first molars to provide efficient slicing of hide. The only parts that can not be digested completely are hooves and some hair. These they regurgitate, to the delight of their den-mates which roll and rub their backs in the material.

Since hyenas eat all parts of the prey, evidence of nocturnal strikes is scant. As a result the hunting skills of hyenas have been overlooked, and the animal has been misjudged and generally underestimated.

In reality, the hyena is a skillful hunter which employs different methods for different, preselected prey. Hyenas are not as fast as cheetahs, but they can chase a wildebeest for about three miles at speeds of up to 37 miles an hour. When they intend to hunt zebra,

a pack of 25 may walk for miles seeking the herd and bypassing more plentiful prey. How they select particular quarry and then communicate their intentions to each other is not known. The numbers and pace employed in the hunt, however, are clearly geared to the defense behaviors and speed of the fleeing prey.

The hyena does make a cackling sound but it does not have much to 'laugh' about. Lions steal their kills more often than the reverse. Since hyenas are chased and cheated so ruthlessly by their competitors, they must compensate by killing more frequently. In order to deter lions in particular, groups of hyenas must stand around lowing, laughing, whooping, and baiting, when they could be relaxing in their favorite warthog hole. As a consequence hyenas earn the awful reputa-

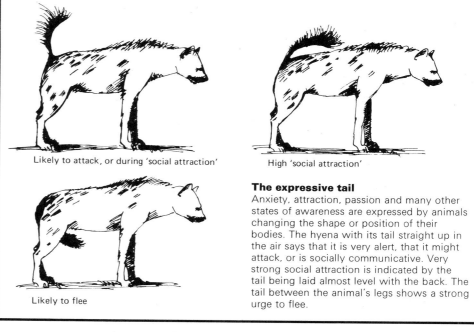

Likely to attack, or during 'social attraction'

High 'social attraction'

Likely to flee

The expressive tail
Anxiety, attraction, passion and many other states of awareness are expressed by animals changing the shape or position of their bodies. The hyena with its tail straight up in the air says that it is very alert, that it might attack, or is socially communicative. Very strong social attraction is indicated by the tail being laid almost level with the back. The tail between the animal's legs shows a strong urge to flee.

Hyena cubs are preyed upon by members of their own species as well as by others, but the tables are turned for the lion above.

tion of insatiable killers and noisy, bad-tempered beasts.

Using a radio-transmitter collar, two American scientists tracked a female hyena and those she associated with minutely for 281 hours. They found that hyenas are active for only 15·8% of the day, and of this short period even less time is devoted to hunting and feeding. They are most active in the early night and predawn hours. Most of the time hyenas can be found lying down or sleeping in holes or near their dens. The dens are networks of underground tunnels dug by other animals and hyena cubs.

Cubs, like the young of all species on the plain, are vulnerable to predators, and hyena cubs are open to attacks by cannibalistic adults of their own species as well. Although female hyenas are larger than males, mothers are not always around to protect their litters, which usually contain just two young. Therefore, cubs have fully developed defense behaviors like squealing, running, digging, and hiding quietly underground.

Hyenas do not attempt to hunt until they are about eight months old, but they can eat meat before this time. They are weaned at one year, when they are fully grown and capable of hunting with the pack.

As in other territorial mammals, the sense of smell is acute. Like the cheetah, the hyena will stop, sniff with urgent attention, and remark grass stalks and other spots previously marked by other hyenas. Instead of applying scented urine like cats, hyenas apply an anal gland secretion, called paste, that smells like soap. After this pasting ritual, they scrape the ground with a forepaw leaving a scent, produced by interdigital glands, in the scratch marks.

Scent marking not only delineates territories but also describe aggressive feelings that hyenas may have toward members of other species and, in the case of males, toward sexually uncooperative females. Since hyenas rely on group cooperation in hunting animals larger than themselves, in-group aggression must be kept down. Scent-marking may be one way of minimizing intraspecific fighting. In this respect and in the fact that they adjust the size of their hunting parties to the game they intend to track, hyenas are like other social carnivores such as wild dogs, lions, and wolves.

Wolf

Wolves are the largest members of the dog family. They have alternately fascinated, terrified, and commanded the respect of human beings. From this wild, hunting dog man bred his best friend (*Canis familiaris*) and some say that the dog, which is able to mate and produce viable offspring with wolves, ought to be considered as a subspecies of the wolf.

The habitat of the wolf is generally pictured as arctic tundra, but wolves have inhabited all zones except tropical rain forest and arid desert. There are still red wolves in northern Florida and Mississippi.

The wolf is the predominant predator of the Northern Hemisphere. Although it was once the ruling predator in tundra, taiga (swampy coniferous forest), steppes, savanna, and forest, man's systematic extermination has insured that the species is rare or extinct in most places. Outside of Alaska, there are few wolves in the United States, and outside of Scandinavia and mountainous parts of Eastern Europe, they are rare on the European Continent. In Asia, they are still common throughout China and Siberia, overlapping the range of the reindeer.

Wolves are social animals, like lions and hyenas. This means they have specific adaptive behaviors that permit close association in hunting and living together. They are carnivorous, although less exclusively than cats. Their diet includes everything from big game, like moose and elk, to earthworms, berries, and grasshoppers in spring.

Sometimes the abilities and dispositions of social carnivores seem contradictory. They have gentle, intelligent, and even fearful responses among themselves or when faced with an adversary like man. But they are capable of extremely aggressive, uncheckable pursuit and attack when taking food, meeting a strange member of the same species, or protecting the young from predators. Normally, wolves are docile. When caught or injured, they are afraid of human beings. When reared from pups, they become loyal pets. This is why it was probably relatively easy for man to domesticate the

*The European Wolf (*Canis lupus*) will refrigerate a kill in the snow for a future meal when prey is scarce in winter.*

wolf, some 12,000 years ago in the Near East. Since then, man has exploited the wolf for its extraordinary tracking and hunting ability, for its strength and friendly companionship. Each of these and scores of other traits, from the fleetness of greyhounds to the diminutive, hairless charm of chihuahuas, have been extracted from the wolf genome by man's selective breeding processes.

Coming from a long line of meat-eaters, the wolf is the descendant of a generalized, carnivore ancestor, called Creodont, which lived in the Northern Hemisphere from 120 to 100 million years ago. This ancestor was common to all modern carnivores, such as cats, bears, civets, dogs, and hyenas. The result of these 100 million years of evolution is a synthesis of physical characteristics, sensory abilities and social ordering that make the wolf a superb hunter, efficient meat-eater, and reliable member of the pack.

A wolf weighs and measures approximately the same as a small man. About 100 pounds and 5·5 feet from nose to tail tip, it is engineered for trotting and running long distances. Ordinarily a wolf trots at four to five miles per hour. When being hunted by man, they can cover 124 miles in a day, but when they are safe, their range is only 15 to 30 miles per day.

Wolves can swim and do not hesitate to follow and even feed upon an animal while treading water. Their massive jaws and chewing muscles, their set of 42 teeth, including 2·75-inch canine fangs, allow them to immobilize prey ten times their own weight. A wolf can clamp its pointed incisors and canines into the nose or rump of a strong bull moose and hang on as the prey whips and tosses it in the air.

The formation of the wolf's front teeth contrasts distinctly with the broad, blunt front teeth of herbivores that are best suited to clipping and pulling stems, leaves, and grass. Cheek teeth (premolars and molars) are also very different in hunter and hunted. Since carnivores generally bolt their food, their cheek teeth are equipped to slice skin and tendon and crush bone quickly. The furious pace of eating is probably to protect the carnivore from attack or loss of quarry to other predators. It is not uncommon to find whole

tongues, livers, and ears in wolf stomachs. The grazers, on the other hand, do not swallow until vegetable material is mashed and ground to satisfaction.

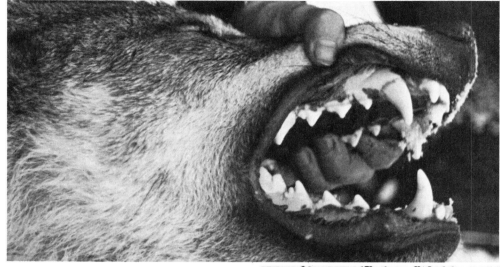

The fearsome jaws and teeth of a wolf (above). Dogs injure and chase prey until it dies of exhaustion and loss of blood (right).

The entire digestive system of the wolf is geared to the feast and famine life, so that they can eat every five to six hours when food is plentiful or fast and live on scraps for two weeks. Their stomachs can hold up to 20 pounds from one feed. They lap up large quantities of blood and water with their long tongues. Everything except five per cent of large meat feasts can be digested and the waste is almost completely liquid. Mysteriously, splinters of bone that are not broken down become wrapped in undigested hair, protecting the intestine from puncture. These 'packages' and other waste excretions are called scats and provide biologists with much necessary information about the diets of the species they study.

Wolf anatomy also provides for extreme olfactory and auditory sensitivity. This permits the animals to locate food and each other across great distances. The long nose warms cold air and provides an extended mucous surface which, combined with nerve connections to the olfactory center of the brain, gives members of the dog family a sense of smell about 100 times as acute as our own. A wolf can detect prey up to one and one half miles downwind. Hearing is similarly well developed, even in high frequency ranges. Wolves respond to human

shouting or wolf howling at distances that may exceed four miles.

When a wolf catches the scent of a deer, moose, or caribou, it veers and trots upwind, until it sees its quarry. Sometimes the scent of the prey will be followed from its tracks, at other times predator and prey confront each other by accident. Wolves stalk in a tense, alert manner, but they do not crouch and slink like cats. As with so many other land predators, they may be deterred by prey that approaches or stands its ground. Adult moose and elk will usually bluff in this way. It seems that wolves, like other hunting carnivores, need the stimulus of a retreating animal to trigger the chase. Normally, pursuit will not exceed half a mile. They will not expend much energy in trying to catch very strong, swift prey. They eat the old, young, sick, or otherwise weakened member of a herd first. In the spring, they eat calves and fawns. In summer, when the herds migrate, they take mice, birds, and even fish. They may eat carrion of their own or other species. They feed first on the prime parts of their kill such as rump, visceral organs, and fat. They return later for the less desirable parts. Sometimes observers, who witness only the first feed, suppose that wolves are wasteful eaters. In fact, wolves cannot afford to waste, and what they do not eat is often cached in the natural icebox around them. Hidden under snow or icy soil, food is safe from vultures, ravens, and summer flies. Food is also hidden when pups cannot finish eating what the adults bring them. When the young beg for food, by licking and gently biting the parents' muzzle, the adult either disgorges fresh meat or immediately goes out to hunt for food. Whole legs of caribou and pieces of other animals are often brought back to pups in the den.

Interestingly, it is not always the mother who makes the most effort in feeding, cleaning, and playing with the pups. An unmated female or a male are just as likely to take up these activities. Communal care of offspring is just one beneficial aspect of pack life. Living in packs, adhering to a fixed social order, is adaptive in many ways. For example, when cutting through the difficult winter wilderness, the pack proceeds in single file, following the leader, which

A European Wolf extracts the last morsel from its prey. Its teeth are formed to aid the quick tearing of flesh from the bones.

is strong enough to break a trail through deep snow to spare other members an unnecessary waste of effort.

There are separate dominance orders for males and females in a pack. According to these hierarchies, each individual occupies a position of greater or lesser freedom of movement and access to food and sex. The top ranking members are called alpha males and females. They are not replaced or displaced except in case of their death or serious injury. Occasionally, a female with new pups will exceed her normal rank temporarily. New members are added to the dominance order as they reach maturity. Play-fighting among pups and juveniles up to two years old helps determine their rank, which could be dominant alpha, subordinate, or peripheral. Imitation of the behaviors of a high-ranking mother can perpetuate dominance from one generation to the next.

A leader sets the pace of the pack. When he moves, the pack follows, and when he rests, all must rest. Taking the initiative in pursuit and attack of prey, control of space, and defense of the group, the leader is usually autocratic but sensitive to the needs and abilities of the pack. Alpha males patrol the group and are first to confront a stranger. The leader may even escort a zookeeper around the cage as he works and see him to the exit when he leaves.

In-pack fighting is rare. It erupts

most often during the mating season. Ritualized threat and submissive gestures are generally sufficient to confirm status positions. In unstable packs, a group of males may taunt a low-ranking scapegoat, which may be injured, driven from the group, or killed, depending on the amount of aggressive tension these males need to express. Submissive and dominant positions are conveyed through body posture, facial expression and tail movements. A threat display consists of staring, listening, and smelling the subordinate. Dominant animals raise their tails as excitement increases. Their foreheads wrinkle, and their ears stand up. They bare their sharp teeth. When the dominant member has gained a show of submissiveness, like crouching with lowered tail and ears, the fight is over. The winner may 'stand across' the forequarters or 'ride up' by placing front feet on the shoulders of the loser.

The roots of social interaction are thought to lie in early feeding and eliminative routines, as well as in play-fighting. Both active and passive submission have their prototype in adult-pup interactions. The active-submissive display between adults echoes the pattern of begging for food. The pup gently mouthes the muzzle of the adult which regurgitates predigested food. The passive-submissive display seems

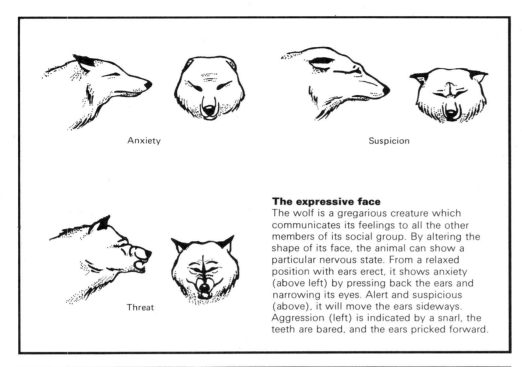

Anxiety

Suspicion

The expressive face
The wolf is a gregarious creature which communicates its feelings to all the other members of its social group. By altering the shape of its face, the animal can show a particular nervous state. From a relaxed position with ears erect, it shows anxiety (above left) by pressing back the ears and narrowing its eyes. Alert and suspicious (above), it will move the ears sideways. Aggression (left) is indicated by a snarl, the teeth are bared, and the ears pricked forward.

Threat

to arise from just the reverse behavior between mother and pups. When still nursing, the mother may stimulate the belly and anal-genital area of her young by nuzzling their underside. This encourages elimination, and the waste of the offspring is eaten by the mother. These behaviors not only show the possible psychological and postural basis of adult interactions but also demonstrate the remarkable conservativeness in exchange of food between adult and young.

Like cats and hyenas, wolves rely on scent marking for communication. They also investigate each other personally at the mouth region to determine when the last meal was eaten and what it comprised, and at the tail end to identify membership in the pack or sexual receptivity. There is a special gland on the dorsal side of the tail that may give cues about relative status and aggressiveness. Sometimes it is easy for human observers to confuse the dominant and submissive animals when looking at postures alone. Scent clues (pheromones) that assist this discrimination are not interpretable by humans. Without more knowledge of scenting, our understanding of certain confrontations may remain ambiguous.

In the frigid wilderness, wolf packs seldom meet each other. If a pack meets a stranger, it will chase or kill it. If a pack comes across a freshly scented marker it will steer away from the hunting area beyond that boundary. After excited investigation of a new scent, the members of the pack will line up to re-mark the station with their own urine.

Along with marking behavior, the familiar wolf howling may reinforce territorial rights. All the functions of howling are not well understood. Howling probably does not call wolves to prey, as was once thought. They are quiet when they stalk, and howling would frighten the prey. After a hunt, howling probably helps stranded wolves relocate their packs. The pitches and styles of calling differ among individuals, and it is quite possible that members learn to identify each other by voice. It is apparent that howling choruses are enjoyable experiences for the members of the pack and as such support the gregariousness essential to the organization of the wolf pack.

PART FIVE

PREDATORS AND THE BALANCE OF NATURE

Man and the animals . their relation in the ecosystem

There are certain traits common to all vertebrate predators. Some of these unifying patterns of anatomy and behavior are sensory acuity, with usually the perfection of one sense for accurate prey tracking; physical strength and weaponry; and some activated and directed behaviors, which we call aggressiveness, for coping with prey.

Predators also have various effective ways of guarding their fertilized eggs and of protecting their young from other predators or adult members of their own volatile species. Avian and mammalian predators also seem able to provide their young with some training in methods of hunting. Whether fish, amphibian, mammal, or bird, predators are often gregarious and distribute their groups over territories to share food equally. To accomplish this they possess certain means of announcing their presence such as smells, colors, calls, active displays, that may flourish into complex patterns of communication in certain species.

It is soon apparent, however, that prey animals also have these characteristics. They have keen senses, physical strength and/or structural defenses, like great speed, agility, or weight; tusks, antlers, and tough hides. They have activated and directed behaviors for coping with predators through avoidance or defensive maneuvers. They care for, protect, and possibly train their young. And they too have territories and can communicate.

So, as in all natural phenomena, things that appear to be opposite, like predators and prey, are actually just dual aspects of one thing. Each is a complementary manifestation of the other, forming a balanced exchange of energy that provides both with life.

The distinguishing feature between predators and prey is not any absolute difference in traits but a difference in emphasis and application of these traits. It is possible that predator and prey species could be distinguished on some scale of relative aggressiveness. Some species would be clearly more aggressive than defensive, which would

*(Previous page) Long-eared Owl parents offer their young a mouse. The otter (right) is an expert swimmer. As well as eating fish it catches small waterbirds. (Far right) The jungle cat (*Felis chaus*) habitually hunts small mammals and birds with great speed and agility.*

show up as higher indexes, and others would be more defensive than aggressive, which would show up as lower indexes. But even if this could be done, it would only codify facts we can readily observe. It would not explain the source of predator-prey behavioral distinctions or interactions.

Why are some species more disposed to fight? Why are some more prone to flight? It may have something to do with genetically determined relative proportions of adrenal gland secretions, called epinephrine and norepinephrine. Emphasis on production of the former may dispose the species or individual to active retreat and emphasis on the latter to attack. There is some evidence that little prey animals, like guinea pigs, are high epinephrine producers and respond to stress with anxiety, and that predatory types, like cats, are high norepinephrine producers and respond to stress with aggression.

Whatever the basis for differences in the ratio of aggressiveness to defensiveness between predators and prey, we are always left with a relative, not an absolute, differentiation. Predation is ultimately defined in the jaws of the victor.

Every animal is both predator and prey in a larger picture. The first link of the food chain is bound to the last in an eternal circle. Every species' position is dualistic. They all eat, grow, and incorporate energy which necessarily gives way to escaping, being caught and eaten, or dying and returning energy to the environment. Even the most successful predators, which seem only to eat, grow, and incorporate energy over a long lifetime must eventually die and disintegrate, leaving their component materials to the plants through the intercession of bacterial decay.

Remembering that the predators, conceptually set off here as a separate group of animals, are really united with all species in a great circular exchange of energy, similar patterns of evolution and behavior that may exist among these predators can be examined. What types of sensory abilities, patterns of aggression, and protection and training of the young, of grouping and communicating have evolved among predators?

Sensory acuity

Different sensory abilities are well-developed in different classes. Fish seem to rely most on the senses of touch and smell; amphibians on touch and vision; reptiles on touch, smell, and in some cases on vision and hearing; birds on vision and hearing, especially in nocturnal types; and mammals on smell, vision, and hearing to pursue the predatory lifestyle.

The environment is important in determining which senses will be emphasized in a particular species. Thus, dark-dwelling bats and cetaceans, so different in their appearances and movement habits, are united in their echolocating abilities. Their sensitive hearing is a highly evolved and specialized extension of the tactile sense that picks up low-frequency vibrations.

Distant touch, the sense that allows us to feel the trembling that travels up the legs of our chair as a bus passes along the street in front of our window, was probably the first sensory system that permitted vertebrates to perceive information about objects not in immediate contact with their bodies. This sense of distant touch was mediated by the lateral line system of early teleosts and selachians.

The lateral line system is a set of sense organs arranged in a line on either side of a fish or larval amphibian. Some of the lateral line nerves have stimulus-transmitting connections to the auditory area of the inner ear,

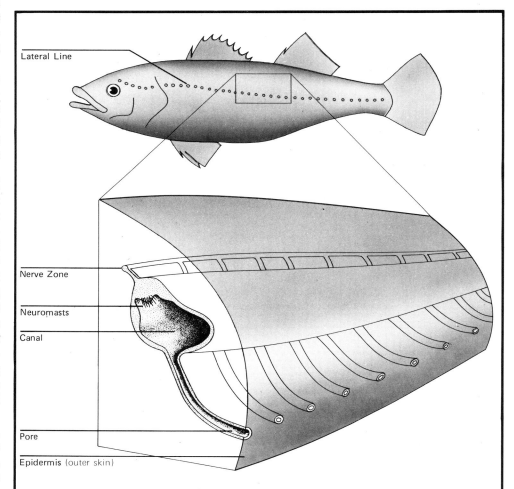

The lateral line system
Many fish have a well developed sense of 'distant touch.' This means that they are highly sensitive to vibration and movement in the water. They have canals of fluid situated in lines down the sides of their bodies and over their heads. These canals are connected to both the nerve zone and the outer skin.

When a disturbance occurs around the fish, this is transmitted through the pores in the skin to the fluid canal which contains neuromasts. These are fine, hair-like growths in the canals which transmit the messages received by the fluid to the nerve zone, which also travels down the length of the fish's body showing how closely perceptions of vibration through the skin and ears are related.

Vibration conduction via the swim bladder and bones of the jaw, and modification of the bladder into a pinched-off area in the ear region in certain modern species show that many tissues coalesced in the formation of the auditory sense. The fact that sensory cells resembling those found in the lateral line are present in the inner ear of modern fishes suggests that lateral line nerves in this region in early fishes evolved in a way to permit more refined vibratory discrimination over a greater frequency range. Thus, species that were once dependent on perception of low frequency vibrations conveyed through water at slow speeds for all distant environmental information, evolved, through time, into other species able to detect higher pitched, faster vibrations that we call sound. Now, several millions of years later certain species of vertebrates of other classes have modified the primitive auditory sense to such a degree that ultrasonic (very fast, short wave, high frequency) and infrasonic (very slow, long wave, low frequency) vibrations can be heard.

Again it is the needs of environment and lifestyle that dictate the evolution of special senses. Therefore, distantly related groups, like sharks and wolves, are sometimes similar in their sensory emphasis, for example in their sense of smell, which shows up as a convergent adaptation to hunting.

In the same way, many birds of prey and mammals have excellent distant and color vision, which may be the result of common arboreal ancestry more than hunting pattern pressures. Although good sight obviously serves modern predators well in the pursuit of prey, it probably did not develop in response to predatory needs. It may have been a response to the need for movement and food-gathering of ancient, insectivorous and herbivorous reptiles. These were the first vertebrates to occupy the tree niche about 100 million years ago and they gave rise to all modern mammalian and avian predators.

Now let us look at the acuteness and specialization of senses among predators of each of the five vertebrate classes of animals.

The Eel spawns in the Sargasso Sea. The elvers go by the Gulf Stream to rivers, which they leave to return to the Sargasso to spawn and die.

Fish

Vision

Although some deep-sea and muddy-water types of fish are nearly blind, most teleosts see well and rely on vision for predation and its avoidance. Fishes living in shallow water, where light penetrates well, have color vision. Certain species of sharks also seem to have color vision.

Dr. Eugenie Clark, testing sharks for their ability to associate different targets with food rewards, accidentally found that Lemon Sharks (*Negaprion brevirostris*) dislike yellow targets, which they turned away from abruptly. Whether or not this would be a reliable shark repellent, even for this species, requires more research to determine.

Fish seem to be able to identify shapes best when these shapes are moving. This helps them to pursue prey and avoid predators. Binocular depth vision is also present in certain species. The pikes (species *Esox*) have overlapping visual fields and thus can see in three dimensions, as we do.

Although we think of the five senses as being separate, they overlap and interconnect more than we realize. The borders of the different senses are not as discrete as they appear. Light sensitivity, which is the essence of vision, is not always limited to the eyes.

Among fishes and certain species of other vertebrates the skin, and the pineal and dorsal brain surface have light-sensitive nerves. Retinal stimulation as well as stimulation of these areas in a fish may trigger rapid movement away from the light source or a rapid change of body color.

Hearing

Just as the border between hearing and touch is hazy, so that between vision and hearing in fish may not be discrete. This overlap, as it occurs in fish, assists them to maintain their equilibrium. Changes in light that stimulate the retina can help orient a fish in its normal swimming posture. And this orientation in relation to the direction of incoming light is accomplished by the inner ear working with the lower part of the retina. If the inner ear is damaged, a fish may swim on its side.

Many fishes can hear and produce noises, using the gas bladder as a sound conductor and resonator. Bones connecting the ear and swim bladder help in the reception of sound. Unfortunately, we do not know much about the uses of hearing in predation, mating and alarm signaling among fishes.

Touch

Nocturnal hunting fishes and selachians, which cannot rely on vision, use their sense of touch to locate food. The lateral line system, described earlier, is

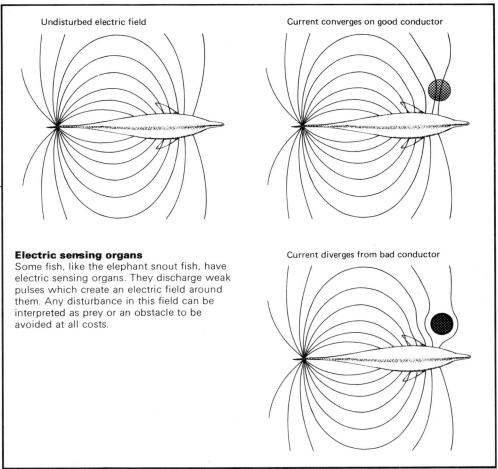

Undisturbed electric field

Current converges on good conductor

Current diverges from bad conductor

Electric sensing organs
Some fish, like the elephant snout fish, have electric sensing organs. They discharge weak pulses which create an electric field around them. Any disturbance in this field can be interpreted as prey or an obstacle to be avoided at all costs.

Sperm Whales (Physeter catodon), *which have no dorsal fin, seen here washed ashore at Cape Schanck, Victoria, Australia.*

the principal receiving organ of touch among fishes. The lateral line organs can perceive frequencies between 16 and 200 cycles per second.

One of the most specialized modifications of the sensory system of the skin is the electricity discharging and receiving organs found in species of eel, ray, mormyrid, and gymnotid fishes. The charge produced by the electric eel (*Electrophorus*), the *Torpedo* rays, and electric catfish (*Malapterurus*) can stun or kill prey. Eels other than *Electrophorus* can produce moderate voltages with which they establish an electric field around themselves. This field extends the sensitivity of the skin outward. If small fish, worms, or insect larvae enter the field, the resulting distortions are felt by the predator.

You can experience a mild form of this by rubbing a plastic balloon on wool and then bringing it near your face. Before the balloon touches your skin, you can feel the static electric field. The fish, like the balloon, carries such a field with it, except that in water its field is much stronger than that of the balloon. It seems that other fish, swimming into the surrounding field of the predator, should be able to sense a change and be warned away from the predator.

Smell

For some species, the sense of smell is more informative than vision, touch, or hearing. The nasal pits of sharks and rays, in particular, are sensitive to odors flushed over the sensitive surfaces of the pits, when water is inhaled. In some bony fishes (species *Icatalarus*, catfish; *Lepomis*, sunfish; *Oncorhyncus*, salmon) there is extraordinary sensitivity to dissolved organic substances. The common eel (*Anguilla*) may be able to detect dilutions of only a few molecules of odorous material in its nasal sacs. Such smell sensitivity guides these fishes to prey and to spawning grounds. Minnows (Cyprinidae) can even produce an alarm substance that warns other members of its species of danger and disperses them in every direction.

Amphibians and reptiles

Predatory amphibians and reptiles may be sensitive to odors also. Smell and the specialized sense of touch for feeling temperature are most important to snakes. Sight is weak in snakes but may be of greater importance in amphibian predators.

James Oliver divides the sensory capacities of the creatures into six categories to show that they have senses that are different from our own.

Smell

Olfaction is classified as a form of chemoreception. The special organs for smell and taste can perceive dissolved chemicals in air and liquid, respectively. The border between these two senses is indistinct, especially among the herptiles. Amphibians have nasal chambers. The sense of smell seems more active in aquatic amphibians and terrestrial salamanders than in toads and terrestrial frogs, which rely on taste to reject unpalatable food. In snakes the focus of the sense of smell is the nasal pits. It is assisted by another receptor called the Jacobson's organ, which is found in the roof of the mouth. Although the snake's tongue does not taste, it explores objects by touching them and bringing small fractions of their substance to the Jacobson's organ for smelling. The rock python, described earlier in Chapter 4 in the act of eating a bushbuck, will flick its tongue in and out over the length of its dead prey.

This sort of chemoreception enables snakes to track their prey. Pythons can find a dead rabbit in a perforated box or buried underground by following a scent trail with their tongues. The tongue and Jacobson's organ are probably also important in tracking down a suitable mate.

Light and heat sensors

Except for the burrowing and some cave-dwelling species, herptiles have light-sensitive eyes. Some have more acute vision in daylight, others are better at night.

Unlike other herptiles, snakes have lidless eyes that are protected by a

Sensory Receptors of Herptiles

1. Chemical receptors in the
   a. nose (below)
   b. Jacobson's organ (below)

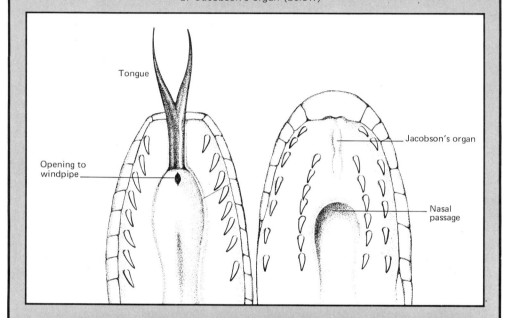

c. tongue (above)

2. Radiant energy receptors in the
   a. eyes (light only)
   b. skin (light and heat)
   c. facial pits of pit vipers (heat)

3. Vibration receptors
   a. ears
   b. lateral line (aquatic larvae and some adult amphibians)

4. Mechanical equilibrium receptors in the
   a. skin
   b. muscles
   c. inner ear

5. Moisture receptors in the skin

6. Pain and hunger receptors in the
   a. skin
   b. internal organs

The receptors in categories 1, 2, and 3 are of main importance.

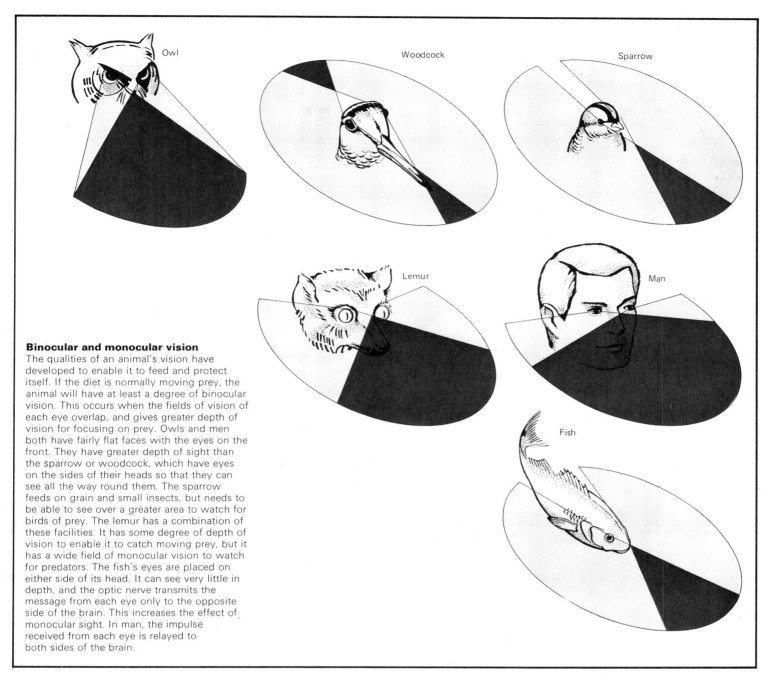

Binocular and monocular vision
The qualities of an animal's vision have developed to enable it to feed and protect itself. If the diet is normally moving prey, the animal will have at least a degree of binocular vision. This occurs when the fields of vision of each eye overlap, and gives greater depth of vision for focusing on prey. Owls and men both have fairly flat faces with the eyes on the front. They have greater depth of sight than the sparrow or woodcock, which have eyes on the sides of their heads so that they can see all the way round them. The sparrow feeds on grain and small insects, but needs to be able to see over a greater area to watch for birds of prey. The lemur has a combination of these facilities. It has some degree of depth of vision to enable it to catch moving prey, but it has a wide field of monocular vision to watch for predators. The fish's eyes are placed on either side of its head. It can see very little in depth, and the optic nerve transmits the message from each eye only to the opposite side of the brain. This increases the effect of monocular sight. In man, the impulse received from each eye is relayed to both sides of the brain.

transparent skin called the brille. The unique external and internal structure of their eyes may be the result of re-adaptation to life above ground, after a long evolutionary period of underground existence, during which snake eyes became degenerate.

Lizards, turtles, and some frogs have color vision, and snakes are probably more sensitive to the longer, red range wavelengths of the spectrum than to other colors.

Binocular vision is particularly important to predators which rely on vision for hunting. The most successful predators of each class of vertebrates, therefore, generally have forward-directed eyes that provide good depth perception. So, like the archer fish, pike, snapping turtle, cheetah, hyena, owl, and man, predatory snakes often have binocular vision. Although it is less important than smell or heat detection, it assists in the location of moving prey.

For prey species, distance perception is not as important as wide-angle range.

Therefore, in contrast to predators, prey animals usually have laterally placed eyes and no binocularity.

Another dimension of radiant energy detection among snakes is the ability to detect light without image formation. This occurs on certain areas of the skin and at the pineal region on top of the head. This is sometimes called the third eye, and it helps the cold-blooded herptile avoid direct, intense, light, which might cause the animal to get too hot. There is probably some light sensitivity in the pineal in humans at early ages. This photosensitivity may be important in triggering hormonal changes for the onset of puberty.

Specialized heat-sensitive organs are found in pit vipers and certain boid snakes. These include rattlesnakes, copperheads, moccasins and pythons, and boas of the Boidae family. The name pit viper is given to this group of snakes because of the heat-sensitive pits found on either side of the head, not because these snakes live in pits.

The facial pits may be sensitive to infrared light, as well as heat. The remarkable sensitivity of these organs permits the snake to detect small prey mammals by their body heat, even at distances greater than one foot. Even temperature differences less than one degree Fahrenheit between the snake's body and that of its prey can be perceived.

Vibration sensors
Hearing is the least important sense in snakes and most other herptiles. However, vibrations in solids and liquids are discerned in other ways. Exceptions to the general deaf-muteness of this category of vertebrates are frogs, certain lizards, and crocodilians, which have well-developed ears and voices that serve important functions in territory delineation and mating.

Salamanders and snakes sense vibrations from the ground that are transmitted via their bones to nerves in the region of the ears.

Birds

Hearing

In predatory birds, hearing is relatively acute. Next to vision it is the keenest sense, especially among nocturnal predators like owls. Apart from assisting in the location of small prey, hearing permits communication between members of the same species, helping them to distinguish their territories and to acquire mates. The pitch range of hearing is probably restricted in each species to the range of its voice.

Vision

The sense of sight is best developed among the vertebrate class of birds. The eyes are very large, and in some cases they exceed the weight of the brain. Generally, so much room in the skull is devoted to the eyes that there is no space for surrounding musculature. Thus, the eyes of birds are generally immovable in their sockets.

In birds with excellent vision, like hawks, the area of greatest visual acuity on the retina, the fovea, is doubled. Presumably the higher concentration of rod and cone cells in this area magnifies images upon the retina. In kingfishers the double fovea is thought to

The Reticulated Python is the world's largest snake (left). The Wedge-tailed Eagle hovers over and scans the ground for prey which it swoops on and carries into a cliff or tree (above).

provide good vision in the alternating mediums of air and water in which the bird must operate.

Binocular vision is good among predatory birds. The visual field overlap is described by an average arc of 50 degrees, compared to the human visual field overlap of 140 degrees. Woodcocks (*Philohela minor*) can even turn their eyes to gain backward as well as forward depth vision.

Herbivorous birds, which are often the prey for raptors, have a much smaller field of binocularity of about 25 degrees of overlap.

Smell and taste

These are both very limited in birds. Certain geese and turkey vultures can smell, but for the most part birds rely on sight and the texture of an object, which the bird will explore with its beak to decide its edibility.

Birds may not have strong senses of smell or taste, but their eyesight is keen. The Bee-eater (left) snatches its prey from the air; the Kingfisher (right) dives to pick small fish from streams; the vulture sights a comrade's circling movements in the air and they join together to finish the hyenas kill.

Mammals

Smell

An acute sense of smell is important in spacing and communication between animals of the same species. Scent-marking behavior in certain mammals serves a similar purpose to the calls used by certain birds to define their territories.

Among cetaceans and higher, or more recently evolved, primates, the sense of smell is reduced or absent. In these mammals, the acuteness of the sense of smell defers to that of sight and hearing, and the olfactory lobes are relatively small.

Hearing

Mammals, as a class, rely heavily on hearing to locate prey in a number of ways. From the high-frequency sensitivity of hunting dogs to the echolocating expertise of bats and cetaceans, this sense is of vital importance to them.

It seems that whenever a sense, like vision, olfaction or hearing, evolves to great sensitivity for the purposes of predation, it also becomes valuable to the species for communication. This linkage of predatory behavior and conspecific communication and grouping through the specialized sense organs, is adaptive because it enhances hunting efficacy indirectly through group cohesion as well as directly through increased acuity. It seems, therefore, that improved acuity fosters gregariousness and gregariousness fosters hunting and defense.

Improved group interaction through keen senses permits longer mother-young relationships during which hunting is learned and perfected, again insuring the survival of the group.

Although we often think of social communication for teaching, warning, directing, and pack tracking occuring through the vocal-auditory system, smell and vision also provide examples of hunting senses deflected to other uses. Visual interpretations of postures and movements of conspecifics as well as olfactory interpretation of scent-marks maintain the group and serve to aid the group's hunting activities and efficiency.

The brown bear is not strictly carnivorous. It will eat roots if prey is not available.

A 28 inch salmon is kid's stuff for an Alaskan Brown Bear (left). They can carry off a 900 pound bison, and can sprint after prey at 30 miles an hour over short distances. The European Wild Cat (above) is the ancestor of the more friendly domestic pet.

Vision

Except in cases of dependence on ultrasonic hearing, vision is always keen among mammalian predators. Some nocturnal predators, like hyenas, have specialized retinas that concentrate all available light. This feature, called the *tapetum lucidum*, is present in vertebrate predators of different classes, including the species of sharks, owls, and the species of cats.

Excellent visual acuity, binocular and color vision have been particularly emphasized in tree-dwelling mammals, which, like birds, must judge distances accurately. Color vision was important to the herbivorous predecessors of man which relied on color perception to distinguish ripe fruit and edible vegetation in the trees. Therefore, man, unlike most carnivorous mammals, inherits good color vision, which he has applied secondarily to the pursuit of prey and later to the breeding of animals and plants for food.

Touch

Although hearing, vision, and smell are certainly the prime senses among predatory mammals, it is interesting to note that all senses, including touch and taste, are viable in all mammals. There are only isolated instances of evolutionary sensory reduction consistent with special environmental needs. For example, certain burrowing mammals have weak sight and some aquatic mammals are blind, such as the Ganges river dolphin *Platanista gangetica*, or have a weak sense of smell.

The generally high sensory viability of the class as a whole, however, indicates one of the important sources of mammalian alertness that has given the class great evolutionary success. Compared to cold-blooded, terrestrial vertebrates, mammals are always capable of activity and swift response. The fact that the mammalian central nervous system is the most evolved among vertebrates, that their high and approximately constant metabolic rate can provide energy for action at any time, plus the fact that all the senses are working make it possible for mammalian behavior to be novel and adapted to specific situations in many cases.

The sense of touch, although considered a less informative channel for mammalian predators, is still strong in skin sensitivity to heat, cold, pain, and pressure. Most mammals, even marine species that have no other body hair, have vibrissae or whiskers that increase tactile sensitivity around the face. Vibrissae are important in prey as well as in predators for navigation and for investigation of food.

All predators have some keen sense or senses to guide them to prey. The sense of touch is the oldest means through which information about the environment has been received. Touch is present in every class of vertebrates but seems to play its most important role in hunting behavior among fish and snakes, which perceive warmth and ground vibrations of relatively distant prey.

Smell and taste were significant evolutionary advancements and remain important in every vertebrate class except birds. The sense of smell allowed increased accuracy of tracking through discrimination of changing distance of prey according to changing intensity of the stimulus. Smell was the first defined sense which could automatically judge time and distance through the proportion or intensity of the stimulus emitted by the target, whether it was food, mate, offspring, or enemy. The acquisition of such keen senses had profound consequences for animal behavior, especially for predators for which accurate perception of distance and judgment of time are most critical. With a sensitivity to the degree of stimulus it is possible to define the self, as distinct from external environment. With gradient senses, time and space are defined as functions of variable stimulation from a fixed source or of continuous stimulation from a moving source.

Acute vision and hearing did not seem to develop until the appearance of the bird and mammal classes. Among avian and mammalian predators, vision and hearing are closely coordinated for maximum information gathering.

Going from fish to mammal through evolutionary time, there has been an elaboration of the central nervous system that makes classifying and interpreting a constant mixture of stimuli from all the senses more possible. Whether or not this increasing ability to cope with diverse stimuli makes mammals and birds better predators than fish, amphibians, and reptiles can be argued both ways. One thing that increased sensory acuity and nervous system development do guarantee, however, is more novelty of behavior and less stereotyped activity.

There are more choices in pattern for the more recently evolved predators, more choices in pursuit of prey, in social signaling, threat, defense, display, and more awareness of the choice process. From our point of view, life seems to be more interesting for the more evolved predator.

Learning and communication

It is not inappropriate to speak about interest in a discussion of predatory behavior. Predators are fascinating to watch in action precisely because they are interested in and intent upon what they are doing. Their actions appear purposive and pointed, not dreamy and diffuse, like those of the grazing prey.
and diffuse, like those of the prey.

In some species, particularly among fish, amphibians, and reptiles, predation seems very mechanical, controlled by innate pathways that are triggered by external stimuli. In other species, especially among birds and mammals, predation is acquired more slowly. Learning and experience and the attentiveness and memory these inputs imply make predation a more intellect-dependent activity than simple gathering and grazing.

Choices must be made by the predator – choice of terrain, type of prey, individual quarry, and method of attack. The scope of variability of these options is closely aligned to nurture and training with the mother.

Natural selective pressure is applied heavily at the point of reproduction and protection of the offspring. Species possessing adaptations that insure protection of eggs or young, whether through structure, as in the tough egg case of the whale shark, or through behavior, as in the defense of dens by female hyenas, will be perpetuated.

Predators of the more recently evolved avian and mammalian classes usually show behavioral instead of just structural adaptations for the protection of young. The cheetah, wolf, hyena, whale, and eagle have all been shown to have some form of single parent, couple, or group methods of supplying food and shelter for their young. And, in contrast to predators in the earlier evolved fish, amphibian, and reptile classes, whose active pursuit of food usually appears fully developed at birth, mammals and some birds train their offspring to hunt.

An important benefit of extended development of the young and pro-

Play is practice for adulthood. Play-fighting will be turned to good use when the lion cubs are faced with hunting for food.

longed nurture by parents is the appearance of 'play' behaviors among juveniles of the same species. Wolf and hyena cubs, eaglets, and children in certain societies test their relative strengths and practice motor skills that will be necessary in adult hunting behavior. Play activities must occur to establish dominance hierarchies, proper sexual orientation, and future parental behavior. Indirectly, then, the acquisition of an extended juvenile period supports efficient predation by perfecting motor skills, and by contrasting and ordering the physical strength, aggressiveness, and mental alertness of the group members, that in turn permits cooperative defense, hunting and eating. They insure that high ranking members of the order, which will mate and reproduce most often, are the ones that possess traits that are vital to the future survival of the group. They provide socialization that will insure the continuance of the extended parent-young relationship itself. How can play insure that important traits for species survival will be passed on?

With eagles and wolves the answer is clear. Competitive play selects out weaklings. Either the weak individual is killed in rough play or is positioned so low in the hierarchy that freedom of movement, i.e., choice of direction, decision to attack, or mating, is seriously curtailed. Sometimes play success is reiterated by parental attention, as when the victorious female eaglet is fed first and given more than her defeated brother.

How can play insure the perpetuation of extended development? When

Play behavior among the young of certain species enables these young to test their strengths and practice motor skills. Play establishes hierarchies, proper sexual orientation and future parental behavior.

the young interact, certain display patterns are learned that will be transferred to courtship and sexual union. These display patterns coordinate both active and passive elements that may continue to be used as dominant or submissive currency throughout the individual's lifetime. Such behaviors include the 'riding-up' versus crouching pattern in wolves and the generalized mounting versus presenting pattern among certain terrestrial primate groups, like baboons, in which males are sometimes predatory.

Forebearance is also learned in play. Inhibition or halting of aggression and protection of the weaker group member must become part of the behavior pattern of each individual in a social hunting group. Learning this control in play will carry over to essential adult feeding, handling, and training of the young. Learning control also insures a minimum of bickering and injury among the adults of the group.

The complexity of play behavior and learning among predators depends on the availability of brain tissue to store and associate experiences and sort and memorize patterns of stimuli. These are the same brain functions that also permit more complex predatory routines.

The evolution of the vertebrate brain can be surveyed briefly by class to show an association between brain development and problem solving ability as related to predatory survival.

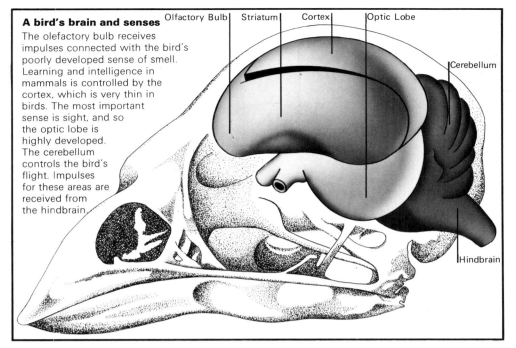

A bird's brain and senses
The olfactory bulb receives impulses connected with the bird's poorly developed sense of smell. Learning and intelligence in mammals is controlled by the cortex, which is very thin in birds. The most important sense is sight, and so the optic lobe is highly developed. The cerebellum controls the bird's flight. Impulses for these areas are received from the hindbrain.

Olfactory Bulb | Striatum | Cortex | Optic Lobe | Cerebellum | Hindbrain

Fish Brain

There are three broad subdivisions of fish: cyclostomata (jawless lampreys and hagfishes); chondrichthyes (sharks, skates, and rays); osteichthyes (bony fishes). Each group has a different general brain construction. The cyclostomes have more primitive brains than the other two groups; that is they have been less changed through evolutionary time. Almost all tissues in the cyclostome brain are devoted to the olfactory bulbs. The light sensitive pineal organ, located on the dorsal (top) midline surface of the brain, is well-developed, with a retina, pigment cells, and a lens-like structure. It is very close to a true focusing eye, peeping through an opening in the cranium that is covered by unpigmented skin.

The brain of cartilaginous fishes, most of which are extraordinary predators, has disproportionately large olfactory and coordination areas and reduced optic areas. This is consistent with the dependence of selachians on smell and continuous circular or figure-eight swimming to follow a scent trail to food.

Bony fishes have the olfactory bulbs reduced and the optic areas enlarged, consistent with their reliance on sight, in most cases, for survival.

All three groups of fishes have a lower brain to body mass ratio than most species in the more recently evolved classes. We associate this fact with the greater stereotypy of fish behavior. Although fish can be conditioned or trained to perform in particular ways and can solve problems

Penguins live in the sparsely populated antarctic continent. As they do not need to fly, their wings have evolved for swimming. The birds come ashore in spring and the female King Penguin (left) lays one egg. Both adults incubate the egg and feed the young.

related to survival (for example, triggerfish, *Pseudobalistes fuscus*, can move small surrounding rocks away from a sea urchin so that it can be approached for eating), the relatively small size of the brain implies that there is minimal learning, associative and memory facility and that fishes rely on automatic patterns of behavior that are released by environmental stimuli.

Amphibian Brain

As predators evolved to existence on land, the lateral lobes of the forebrain (smell brain) enlarged. This area is also called the cerebrum or cerebral cortex or hemispheres. In amphibians there is the first evidence of nervous tissue mixed in the epithelial layer (pallium) that partially covers this area of the brain.

This change, plus enlargement of the spinal cord in the neck and pelvic region accompanied the transition from fins to limbs, from life in water to life on land. More complex movements could be achieved without any significant alteration to the responses to environmental stimuli that characterized the fish stage.

Reptilian Brain

The cerebral hemispheres are further enlarged in reptiles with the appearance of a new area of tissue (neopallium) on the roof of the cerebrum. Nerve cells begin to be present on the outer wall of the neopallium in crocodilians, which are the first predators with a true cerebral cortex. Also for the first time, 12 pairs of cranial nerves are present instead of ten as in fish and amphibians.

The reptilian brain has a relatively large olfactory area and cerebellum, but a relatively small optic area. This corresponds to the emphasis,

among reptiles in general, on olfactory function and complex movements for feeding, mating and breed exclusively on land.

Sight and hearing remained less developed, except among certain small reptiles which began to live in trees about 70 million years ago. These arboreal reptiles had certain mammal-like anatomical and functional features. One of these was faster translation by the brain of stimuli into motor reactions.

Avian Brain

In birds the cerebral hemispheres develop inward into the lateral ventricles (spaces) in the brain. This type of cerebral cortex is called the hyperstriatum and provides for diverse but invariable patterns of avian behavior. The optic lobes are generally enlarged. Predictably, the cerebellum, the part of the brain controlling balance and coordination, is highly developed in flying birds and less developed in flightless ones.

Mammalian Brain

The greatest elaboration of the neopallium, or mantle of grey matter covering the cerebral hemispheres, is seen in mammals. This new brain tissue first evolved among mammal-like reptiles in response to the pressures that living in trees created. It was selected for the faster transmission of sensory and motor impulses.

A censoring mechanism developed in the smell brain, which originally permitted selective response to olfactory stimuli. This area further evolved to take over censorship for other areas of the brain, as adaptation to tree life demanded a reduction of reflex responses to stimulation which increased in the more highly developed and discriminating senses of vision and hearing.

The *corpus callosum* is present in placental mammals. It is a commisure of concentrated nerve tissue between the two halves of the brain and it relays information between them. Each hemisphere controls the opposite side of the body. It is among the partially predatory early hominids (australopithecines) that dominance by one side of the brain probably first appeared.

Beef in an abbatoir in Aberdeen, Scotland. Men may not consider themselves predators but they are one of the most voracious.

Man as a Predator

The question of whether or not sensory and nervous system elaborations, juvenile play, learning, and group co-operation produce better predators cannot be answered without looking at man.

Man supposedly embodies the most highly evolved sensory-intellectual-social package of adaptations. Certainly man has been an active, hunting predator, living regularly by the consumption of members of other species, during certain periods of his history.

Man belongs to an order of mammals, Primates, the species of which are typically adapted to tree-dwelling and herbivorous diets. Most prosimians, monkeys, and apes live exclusively by eating the vegetable materials found in the arboreal, and sometimes terrestrial, environment – leaves, buds, fruit, flowers, pollen, nectar, insects, and shoots, roots and grasses on the ground.

It is probable that man's social and hunting way of life developed from that of the terrestrial, group-living apes of the Miocene period (about 15 million years ago). Like modern baboons, these ancestors of ours were probably savanna-woodland roamers, which ate grasses, stems, roots, berries, fruit, and insects. Their group cohesiveness was survival-adaptive in confrontations with predators and may have been predicted on social ordering established through play and maintained by ritual threat display and submissive adult interactions.

The dominant males of such early ground-dwelling primate groups were herbivorous, like their fellows, but may have taken weak, young prey, when they came upon it in the bush. Such 'passive predation' has been documented for modern species of terrestrial primates, like the ape *Pan troglodytes* (chimpanzee) and the old world monkey, species of *Papio* (baboons). The large male baboon may seize a baby gazelle or young monkey of another species, kill and eat it. Chimpanzee males have been seen cooperating in the ambush of a colobus monkey; one of them acted as decoy, while the other attacked from behind. The males may share such a kill, and sometimes members of the group will beg for food with an outstretched, upturned palm.

Although this does not constitute a regularized pattern of predation, the fact that a social organization existed, with strong and aggressive males capable of taking prey, probably strongly predisposed our ancestors to social hunting.

George Schaller and Gordon Lowther suggested that some of the same ecological pressures that made other carnivores of the African plain predators also made the emerging hominid a hunter. Robert Ardrey, in 1961, emphasized the innate potential for aggression and described tool use, which was almost certainly present even in early herbivorous anthropoids. Modern chimpanzees use leaves as water sponges and twigs as termite probes. This tool use could have worked together with aggressive instinct to stimulate man into being the only fully predatory primate.

The first hominid, *Ramapithecus*, was probably a herbivore, and like modern herbivorous, terrestrial anthropoids, he probably possessed the behavioral potential to hunt and may have done so from time to time. The later hominid, *Australopithecus*, may also have been primarily vegetarian, but evidence of tool use is more reliable for this genus, and the tool kit probably had already been associated with killing. It would not be surprising if the first experiments with this valuable insight were tested out within the early hominid group itself, with strong males occasionally discovering that rocks or long bones augmented the strength of an angry outburst to the point of murder.

Intraspecific internecine behavior among primates has been documented, and has less to do with predation than with competition between males for dominance and territorial or harem control. Hanuman langur males and also male chimpanzees have been observed to kill and eat conspecific young, which often belong to other groups. Without suggesting that murder and cannibalism were or are modal behaviors among anthropoid vege-

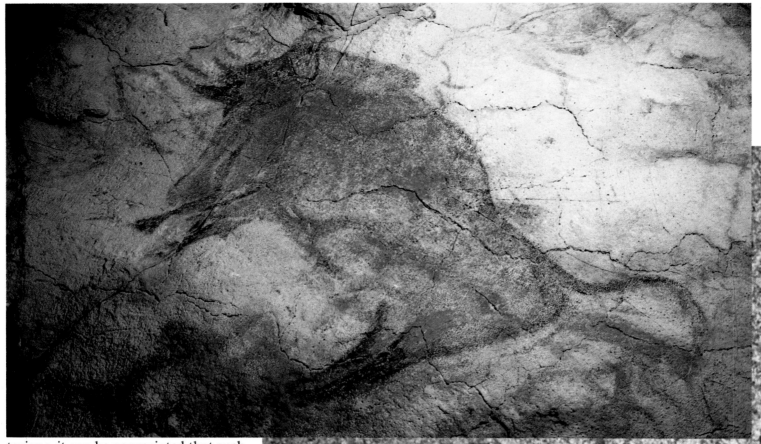

tarians, it can be appreciated that such violent eruptions could imply the potential for the beginning of regularized predation.

Now that some of the predisposing conditions of hominid predation have been mentioned, can the determining causes be identified? A radical shift in diet for a group is generally based on a change in food availability or on implicit recognition of the superiority of a new food source through improved health, activity and survival of the members of the group.

Both of these determining conditions could have been present at the time of hominid predatory emergence. Drought, that cast miocene apes out of the dwindling forest woodlands, could have continued to pressure herbivores sharing the plain. It is very likely that the caloric potency of meat was discovered at about that time.

And how could such a discovery be made? Why was it made by the hominid and not the occasionally carnivorous ape or monkey?

Perhaps the discovery was made possible by the hominid's more evolved associative brain centers. Perhaps because the hominid's juvenile development was slower than that of any other land mammal, there was more time to play and learn, not only with the mother but with adult males and even with members of other species.

Anthropoid juveniles of many spe-

(Above) A prehistoric painting of a charging bison, found in a cave in Altimira. The primitive paintings of a crocodile hunt (right) were found on rock in Zimbabwe.

cies today can be seen to be excellent observers and imitators. Grzimek tells of a game warden in Serengeti who saw young baboons play-riding antelopes. Some films of baboon and new world monkey behavior have captured adolescents of these groups investigating and teasing a bushbuck and large lizard, respectively. Jane Goodall observed and photographed young male chimpanzees mimicking the posture, walk, and display patterns of a chosen 'ideal' model male adult.

Probably the offspring of ancient hominids showed all these abilities to observe, play, investigate, and imitate. Possibly they even watched the felid carnivores stalk and pounce on their prey. With the powers of mimicry, tool use and highly novel behavior at their disposal, early hominids, especially the males, whose larger size and greater strength was probably already genetically determined as in other terrestrial primate groups today, can easily be visualized turning their aggressive capabilities to imitation of the great hunting mammals of the plain.

Imitation of other species is not too far-fetched a notion for the synthesis of human predation. Certainly the broad scope of hunting techniques and adaptations borrowed from other predators, once man had become an established hunter, can be recognized. Stalking like the stealthy cats, wearing the skins of predators for camouflage, dangling lures at fish the way snapping turtles do and even using predators, like hawks and dogs, extend hunting prowess. Similarly, the nearest predecessors of man, australopithecines and other species of *Homo*, must have founded their first cooperative predatory efforts on imitative learning based on the behaviors of social carnivores and other predators around them.

In man it is supposed there is the highest evolution of the sensory-intellectual-social matrix. What really exists is a capacity for learning many behaviors and ordering these behaviors in new ways. This made man a very unusual and versatile predator, although his predaceous behaviors were not genetically programmed. With good memory, and the ability to discriminate relative importance of observed data and to determine appropriate responses, the early hominid could tem-

porarily incorporate new routines into his repertoire and eliminate them if they were not successful. All mammalian land predators must be able to do this to some extent. For instance, cheetah cubs seem to show stalking behavior spontaneously; they must learn where and when to use this innate behavior to become successful hunters.

The fossilized remains of animals at several of the South African australopithecine sites seem to indicate that these early hominids were predators of baboons. Interestingly, most of the baboons seem to have died from a frontally-delivered blow to the side of the head. This seems to show that the ancestors of modern man were already right-handed. Why left cerebral hemisphere dominance seems so early to have become part of the hominid genetic heritage is unknown.

Early man probably did not compete with social hunting carnivores of the hyaenid and canid families which were nocturnal and crepuscular, res-

pectively. Man, as a hunter of large game, probably competed to a small degree with the solitary hunting cats, like the leopard and cheetah, and perhaps to a somewhat greater degree with the diurnal, and more social, plains predator, the lion.

Whether or not bone accumulations found at australopithecine sites actually should be credited to this hominid's hunting activity is often debated. Some paleontologists and paleoecologists, like Dr. Brain and Alun Hughes, suggest that these accumulations are the result of hominid plus other carnivorous mammal activity, including that of hyenas and leopards.

Once the value of projectile weapons and fire had been appreciated, early man became a super-predator and incorporated more and more of the systems he observed working for other species into his hunting method and tool kit. He experimented with lures like the one he saw on serpents' tails, with gaffs that copied the shape of jag-

equal amounts of most vegetable materials, and paleolithic man soon recognized the fast appetite relief afforded by meat, as well as the value of animal skins to sustain body warmth and fats to burn for light in dark northern caves.

Paul Martin and Arthur Jelinek explained why it is probable that the pressures of the early Pleistocene environment caused old stone age man to overkill herds of large mammals. Before the principle of sustained yield through domestication was appreciated, many species such as horses, mastadon, mammoth elephants, camels, sloths, and giant bison of the New World became extinct.

Man used fire to burn the pasture grasses and force herds to areas where they could be hunted easily. These unwary prey of the New World were unused to the new immigrant and predator, man. They could be driven over a cliff or into muddy swamps, and a whole herd of bison or elephant might be killed for the consumption of a few.

Man and the Predators

Generally, predators were exempt from this early burst of human predation, but as man perfected domestication of animals for his moderated and systematic consumption, more predators became the targets of his hunting activity. The fact that man had to learn methods of predatory restraint and incorporate these methods into his cultural tradition emphasizes the recency and novelty of his predaceous phase of existence. All other predators have long established genetic or environmental restraints that make overkill virtually impossible under normal circumstances.

Man, on the other hand, has no obvious anatomical or behavioral inheritance specific to predation – no claws, venom, enormous strength or great swiftness, no blade-like teeth, or super-scenting ability, no sense tailored to the dimensions of a particular prey, the way ultrasonic sniping of a bat is to the form of a moth or tiny minnow darting in darkened waters.

Staying generalized in structure and open to almost complete novelty of behavior, man has gone through many

ged fish teeth, and arrows poison-tipped with toxic plant extracts or venom, like the fangs of reptilian predators.

Dabbling mud and vegetable pigments on his skin, feathering himself like the birds of prey, man developed methods of camouflage. Gradually his cultures formed tools and ideas. The heritage of herbivorousness joined the imitative innovations of hunting. Tools of the herbivore became weapons of the carnivore. Male dominance and strength, that had protected the herbivorous group gathering in the plains, turned to the needs of predation.

The behaviors of predatory animals were idealized, and their styles of hunting and temperamental attributes were transmuted to human values. The sacred animal ancestor, the mascot and the idol appeared. For hunting man, these animal totems were predators. Later, for pastoral man, the idols were grazing, domesticated types.

Naturally, many of the tools of pre-

Man attributes mythical qualities to animals whose characteristics are unknown. The early illustration above leaves no doubts about the artists' fear of monsters of the deep.

dation were invented by and are unique to man, but natural sequences like the recoil of tethered branches when they are released, lightning causing fire, and the activities of other species were always available to suggest new traps, weapons and ploys. Man became an excellent predator, probably induced to perfect his methods by the pressures of changing climate in the areas to which he had migrated.

About ten to 12 thousand years ago, the glacial ice sheets advanced and man was not only less able to find vegetable material to round out his diet, but was also finding that herbivorous game was growing scarce.

Man needed food and more skill to obtain it. The weather grew colder, fewer plants were available, and man needed more calories to stay warm. Meat can provide more calories than lifeway stages in his development – gathering, hunting, domesticating, and cultivating. Man comes from no long line of carnivorous trackers, as do wolves, or from skilled voracious raptors, as do eagles; he was a predator only briefly, by evolutionary time standards, and has just recently (4,000–5,000 years ago is 'just recently' by the evolutionary clock) gained control of this pattern. Now he hunts with restraint and for recreation; his livelihood depends on more peaceful methods of other-species consumption. As a breeder and cultivator, man's values and their embodiment in animal mascots changed.

When man learned to domesticate plants and animals, he did not lose his hunting knowledge. Some groups of men remained hunters, like the Eskimo, even after most peoples had switched lifeway. For the hunter-turned-domesticator, insured of food through livestock and grain reserves, predators became the challenging and profitable new prey.

Man learned that hunting behaviors need not be applied to the aims of predation only but could be applied to exploitation as well. The distinction is that the aim of predation, by definition, is always procuring food, and exploitation is using parts of and only sometimes also eating the prey.

Predators were hunted by man for their economically valuable parts – skins for prized clothing; blubber for oil; bones and tusks of many marine mammalian predators for tools, souvenirs and trinkets of every description. And again, extending the definition of predation to include consumption of prey for purposes other than food, man overkilled and became a superpredator.

It seems that every innovation in a way of life is exaggerated at its beginning, until the limits of its use become more than obvious. Then, man accommodates his methods to his environment, seeking a fair surplus rather than a surfeit of return for his effort.

During this recent period in man's history as an exploitative predator, at least 50 species were extinguished. Most of these were not predators, however. Of the ten predatory species discussed in greatest detail in this book, eight are now endangered, either

The tools and venom with which bushmen hunt were adapted from animals' natural weapons.

through direct exploitation and planned decimation or through sacrifice of natural ranges to advancing civilization.

Domestication, cultivation, industrialization, and urbanization changed and cut the wilderness, then slowly poisoned the rivers, air, soil, and sea. Whether or not man will have the chance to rebound in proper balance from his recent experiments in his way of life remains to be seen.

How and why have predators suffered overkill at the hands of the civilized, part-time hunter?

Often the explanation is fear. Man, who once imitated predators, came to fear their ways and appetites, when he had learned to cultivate his animals and harvest them like crops. Absorbed in a new and sheltered existence of domestication, man no longer competed with or understood so well the natural habits of predators. He kept away from them and they from him, until human numbers grew and confrontations between man and predators became inevitable.

Even now, ignorant man may interpret the normal display of strength and aggressiveness shown by a predator in pursuit of food as something evil or vicious. He has confused his impression of predaceous behavior with feelings of anger and savagery that may precede his own violent attacks upon conspecifics or members of other species. In so doing man has falsely assumed that there is justice in killing predators.

Another explanation of man's slaughter campaigns against predators has to do with the damage it is feared they could cause to livestock, crops (some predators like bears, jackals, and coyotes will eat fruit, berries, honey, and grass) and human life. In

many cases these fears are rationalizations.

Man passed through his great hunting stage, and tore down his predatory idols. It was no longer survival adaptive to emulate predators; their once esteemed qualities are now maligned.

Cultural traditions provide every group of people with evaluative formulations about animals. Through folklore and fairy tales, in the idiom that is taken for granted, each society insures that its members will internalize a 'table of animal values,' as Bernard Neitschmann calls it. In our culture, wolves, bears, snakes, hyenas, and bats may be judged ferocious, sneaky, dirty, and dangerous. Fawns, chipmunks, beavers, rabbits, ducks, lambs, cows, and horses, on the other hand, are gentle, sweet, industrious, charming, and reliable. Nietschmann calls this gradient the 'Bambi factor,' after the endeared cartoon fawn. But why have we endeared gentleness? Why do predators come up short of human charity?

Cultures prescribe certain views of animals partly to reinforce the elimination of types considered to be threatening pests – wolves, certain raptorial birds, the large hunting cats, killer whales – and partly to show people which behaviors are most desirable and fit the needs of the society. Like all prejudices, fixed ideas about animals tend to be accepted as indisputable truths. This is adaptive up to a point because it provides for some control of human behavior.

In an overcrowded society, in a society that need not emphasize its aggressiveness in order to survive, gentleness, as demonstrated by certain patterns in other species, will be idealized. In the past and in certain places today, evaluating and sanctifying certain animals, ascribing supernatural

The ducklings (above right), young duikerbok (centre right), baby rabbit (below right) and koala bears (far right) are some of the animals that receive human approval. Illogically, men believe that animals symbolize human character traits. Certain myths and beliefs in every culture praise and glorify some animals, and reject and despise others. In western societies, meat-eating animals are given negative qualities, such as slyness in foxes, and voraciousness in wolves. Grass- or bark-eating animals are generally given good qualities, such as gentleness in lambs. Bernard Nietschmann described this phenomenon as the 'Bambi factor', after the Walt Disney cartoon animal.

The fox (above) and the owl (left) have hunted their prey and can feed their young, but they too are prey to larger and faster animals, including indiscriminate humans.

powers to them, serves another adaptive function. The sacred animal of the tribe is taboo. It may not be killed or eaten. It passes its special powers from generation to generation of the group, which may regard it as a mythological ancestor. This practice spares various species over any given area occupied by several tribes, and no totem species can be overkilled. However, this function, ecologically important as it may have been at one time, has probably always been secondary to the psychosocial function of 'adaptive emulation.'

Replacing superstition with science did not eliminate fanciful evaluations of animals but added many new utilitarian evaluations. With improved technology, the exploitation of more parts and types of animals became possible and profitable. The value of each species began to be reckoned according to its economic importance.

It seems so normal to view animals as servants of man that we have difficulty imagining another orientation.

As children we hear stories about the obedient and helpful sheep dog, the chickens busily producing eggs for our breakfast, cows giving milk, horses and oxen ploughing fields for our corn. For a while, we may not realize that animals do not exist simply because the superior species needs them.

Although hunters and gatherers, like the South African bushmen and certain tribes along the Orinoco River in South America, seem more anthropomorphic in their descriptions of animals, they actually recognize the separateness of the lives and activities of other species. They credit the adaptive behaviors, personalities, knowledge, and talents of these species. These people do not claim intelligence and motive as their exclusive domain.

Some men, however, do claim this exclusivity. They subject other animal species, and indeed other groups of men, to their service, because they believe that these species and groups have no purposes of their own.

Predators, especially, fall into this category because these wild types often do not exhibit any apparent usefulness to man or woman. Why should there

be so many owls, for instance?

Perhaps the utilitarian point of view makes us ask questions that do not merit answers. Nevertheless we supply answers with emotional, imaginary and 'ecological' explanations that allow the animal on trial some personal quality or broad environmental value for acquittal. Thus, owls are wise and have magical powers. Eagles are courageous and immortal; foxes are cunning; monkeys and apes are comical; poisonous snakes keep down the rodent population. Whether or not these explanations hold any truth, they point out the need for a self-centered justification of the diversity of animal life.

Now, however, in the words of Jacques Cousteau, 'man will no longer be able to be as limited, as utilitarian, and uncomprehending' about the intrinsic value of each species and the value of the balanced interaction of many species. The work of Cousteau and other animal behaviorists provides that man 'will no longer believe in the "ferocity" and "malevolence" of "underwater monsters"' or other species, but that he should confront and contain his own ferocity against them.

Exploitation and conservation

Strictly speaking, all whales are predators, although many of the large baleen species are more like grazing herbivores, peacefully vacuuming tons of tiny invertebrates, collectively called krill or plankton, out of the sea.

Useful, plentiful whales were hunted by man for many centuries. Their oil for fuel, cooking fats, and recently for the manufacture of hormones; their baleen for corset stays and umbrellas; their spermaceti for fine wax candles; and ambergris for perfume were some of the resources and products that made them coveted game.

With the introduction of the explosive harpoon, by 19th-century Norwegian fishermen, the contest was over between men and whales. New methods for hacking and sorting carcasses quickly were developed, and whale exterminating factories hit the high seas in the form of ships fitted to dispatch a 60-ton blue whale in one hour, and capable of taking 31,000 of them in one year.

Since 1944, whaling nations like Japan, Norway, Holland, South Africa, England, and U.S.S.R. have agreed to curtail their exploitation. Now, no more than 16,000 blue whales or their equivalent may be taken each year. But, the blue whale, the largest creature that ever lived, equal in weight to 17 elephants, is nearly extinct.

Some of the predators now endangered are the same ones that have been used traditionally by man to assist him in the hunt. Hawks and falcons were and are still sometimes used to hunt game birds. In fact, the young of these species are often taken from their nests, to accustom them to handling for the sport of falconry, which is growing more popular in western parts of the United States.

If raptorial birds are tamed, they do not compete successfully with their wild conspecifics for game, when they are set free. However, most of the birds

Men have exploited the seas for hundreds of years. The hunting of whales has become highly mechanized, particularly since the 19th-century invention of the explosive harpoon. Factory ships are equipped to parcel up a 60-ton whale in one hour.

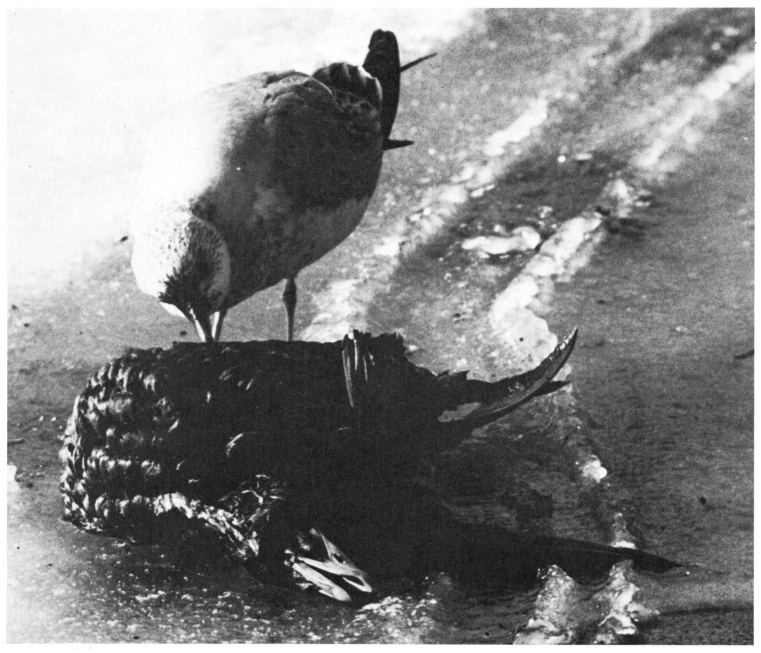

taken for this sport are never set free and never gain the opportunity to hunt or reproduce freely. This form of interference with the species, although too small alone to cause endangerment, if combined with direct hunting of the raptors, encroachment upon their wilderness, and the use of pesticides, which increase shell fragility and may disrupt mating behavior, substantially reduces their chance for survival.

The raptors, both in North America and on other continents, are really not harmful to man, in spite of the bounties placed upon them. The many beneficial qualities of birds of prey should make utility-minded man anxious to protect them, even if ecology-minded man is not yet sufficiently powerful or sophisticated in his arguments to do so.

Leslie Brown says that of 89 diurnal raptors in Africa, 37 are beneficial to

Massive quantities of oil have been spilt and washed from tankers onto the surface of the sea, damaging the natural habitat of fish and birds. The oil-coated bodies of birds are frequently washed onto the seashores.

man, 39 are neutral, and 13 are potentially, though in fact rarely, harmful to man's domesticated animals. Similarly, in the north-eastern United States, owls, considered separately from other birds of prey, show 20 out of 31 species beneficial, eight neutral, and three fish-eating types potentially harmful.

Beneficial species of raptors are those that take rodents, snakes, and insects which may be harmful to man and/or his crops or pastures. The neutral species of raptors take bats, lizards, frogs, and small birds. At times they may be viewed as beneficial, as when they eliminate fruit-eating bats or grain-eating weaver birds. But their good deeds are cancelled by others, as, for example, when they eliminate valuable insect-eating lizards and snakes.

Potentially harmful species, like Martial Eagles and ospreys, may take lambs and edible fish, but unless their numbers are excessive, they pose no great competitive threat. Verreaux's Eagles, which may also pluck lambs from flocks, more than compensate for

an occasional raid by satisfying their normal dietary urge, which is for grass-eating hyraces. Shepherds permit the Verreaux its transgressions because they know that by keeping down the number of hyraces, the eagle provides their flocks with more forage.

Although snakes are not conspicuous hunters, like birds of prey, their predatory ways have also proved useful to man. Snakes catch insects, amphibians, and rodents. Non-poisonous species have been kept on farms and in warehouses and holds of ships to catch mice and rats. A story is told of African villagers who feared and killed large constrictor snakes, until someone realized that the snakes could be tethered and used to capture game. The exploitation of snakes for entertainment, skins, and food is not so severe as to threaten their survival, but changes in their natural habitat which are the in-

Protection from predation by wolves has meant that man has pushed the wolf into the most inaccessible regions of the world. The leopard's skin was prized for fur coats.

evitable consequence of the expansion of our own species may reduce them after all.

Other reptilian predators, like the marine turtle, are not too visible in their predatory habits and do not interfere with man through these habits. Yet these are endangered because they possess something that man wants and takes without restraint – their eggs. Man and omnivorous species that have been introduced to islands where these turtles spawn, eat the eggs and loot the rookeries at every season.

The more obvious predators, like the great cats, are also in danger of extinction. Young cheetahs, trained to hunt by their mothers, were once used by Indian and Persian Princes to bring down ungulate game. For more than 25 years now, these exquisite hunters have been rare or absent in Asia, and

*The Green Turtle (*Chelonia mydas*) is found in warm seas. The eggs of the turtle have been highly valued by men, and preyed upon to the point that these animals have become an endangered species. The Green Turtle's breeding grounds in Malaysia are now protected.*

Dwindling homelands
The map (right) shows the diminishing areas of the world in which the lion, the cheetah and the tiger now live. The tiger used to be found in most areas between Turkey and China. Now it is limited to south-east Asia and India, with small groups remaining in Iran and Manchuria. The plains and savanna of the African continent and south-west Asia are the extent of the cheetah's habitat. The lion once ranged widely through Africa and India, but is now only found below the Sahara Desert in Africa, and in a tiny area in India known as the Gir Forest. The male lion below has a meal of its favorite prey, a wildebeest, which is one of the large, grazing animals found in the savanna.

Arctic Circle

CHINA

AFRICA

ARABIA

INDIA

Equator

Indian Ocean

Lion

Tiger

Cheetah

they would have disappeared in Africa also, if not for the Serengeti, Kruger, and Nairobi Park reserves.

Through indiscriminate hunting and curtailment of woodland-grassland habitat by the plough, lions and tigers also have become seriously endangered in Asia. Native cattle have overgrazed many areas, making the wild game of the carnivores scarce. For the past century, lions have been protected in one small area called Gir on the Kathiawar Peninsula in India. There the herdsmen tolerate a lion's occasional predation upon their cattle because they acknowledge their imposition on the lion's territory, and that they are taking fodder from the game that lions need for food.

Of all predators, the canids have been trained most often for man's use, and yet wolves, who are the immediate relative of man's faithful companion and servant, have almost been wiped out by man in the northern hemisphere. Wherever he cleared forests for settlement, wolves were exterminated. It was feared they would attack children and valuable livestock. Wolves were pictured as scheming and hungry for human flesh, just like the one which ate grandmother in the well-known northern European fairytale.

Where wolves have been decimated, grazing herds have increased in numbers. The elk in Yellowstone National Park in Wyoming, for instance, roam unchecked now by wolf predation. The elk's feeding habits exhaust the vegetation, and periodically they starve. As a result, the numbers of elk are more severely reduced than if their population had been controlled by regular culling by predatory wolves.

Both the United States and Soviet Union have had long-standing wolf-hunting campaigns. The Eastern European drive has continued into recent times. Thirty years ago, 42,600 wolves were destroyed by traps, poisons, and aerial assault. Fifteen years later, only

8,800 were killed, reflecting the decline in numbers of the species, and the distances where they now live.

It has been suggested that predators are worthy of man's protection, that they are of greater use to man and all nature alive than dead, and that they deserve an equal chance to live, regardless of man's evaluations. It is undeniable, however, that predators are aggressive and that the same structures and behaviors, well-adapted to predatory survival, such as the stalk, chase, and attack, strength, appetite, claws, leap, lash, and kill, may be provoked for use against man or his possessions. Having been selected through evolutionary processes, for aggressiveness and all the attendant behaviors of predation, the predator, like a cocked gun, can at certain times, under certain pressures, be triggered against the wrong object. But generally their fierceness is measured and appropriate to their needs, and they do not overkill. Predators are undeniably ferocious, but they do not contrive their violence. In natural habitats their populations cannot grow in disproportion to other species, so their needs cannot undermine the existence of other animals. With his ability to restore or reconstruct environments for endangered species, with his ability to study their reproductive biology and diet, man may halt the imminent extinction of several species.

From the utilitarian point of view, this would be most profitable. Scientists have much to learn from the natural history and physiology of predators. How do bats produce their ultrasonic pulses? What are the neurological networks that permit them to echolocate their prey in the piercing jabber? How do whales and migrating birds hear low frequency infrasounds across thousands of miles? And how do these sounds help them navigate? What interaction of systems permits the brains of dolphins and whales to function well during long, deep dives? How can a huge mammal like the blue whale tolerate two hours without air? How can a shark tolerate its uremic tissues? And then there are the questions specific to predatory lifestyle it-

Pelicans sometimes co-operate in catching shoals of fish. A large number of birds surround the prey and then share the catch.

self. How much of stalk, chase, and kill is learned? How much aggression is innate? Why are most raptorial birds monogamous? Why do wolves form close-knit family groups? And how really did man become a predator?

Obviously, there is an enormous natural resource in living predator species, a resource that may supply us with more understanding and power of control over our universe than delving into atoms has given us already. Living animals and organic webs of interacting species are really super-systems of atoms and molecules that have been built up through inconceivable spans of time. At this point, man is only

guessing about the rules and priorities followed by nature to 'create' these living systems through time. We know laws of chemistry and physics, and we have a theory of natural selection, but what we know is constantly being amplified or altered.

Many scientists hold that, as Paul Martin states, 'extinction is not an abnormal fate in the life of a species . . . The fossil record . . . is replete with extinct animals that were sacrificed to make room for new and presumably superior species.'

This view may be correct, but it may also be perverted to sustain the apathy that exists toward dying or recently

extinct species. People could reason that *Homo sapiens* is evidently superior, so why save other species not strong enough to survive? Is this not simply the law of natural selection? Those who can, survive and perpetuate their genes, their structures, their behaviors; those who cannot, do not.

But should we see species as large scale equivalents of individuals, with a birth, lifespan, and death? From our self-centered vantage, it seems obvious that this is 'the way things are,' just the way it seemed obvious at earlier points in human history that all the stars and planets revolved around the earth and that man could never fly because that

was 'the way things were.' We must be open to the point of view that there is no finality in our present understanding of evolutionary biology.

Many conservationists hold that, as Roy Pinney states, 'the death of a living creature may be sad, but it is a fact of life. . . . The extinction of an entire species is, on the other hand, a direct and absolute contradiction of existence. It is not a part of life . . .'

Which view is correct? Martin's: 'Extinction . . . is not an abnormal fate in the life of a species,' or Pinney's: '. . . extinction of an entire species is . . . not a part of life . . .'?

We must answer that species do appear and then sometimes change in appearance and behavior or are supplanted completely by other species. Normally this process takes millions of years, not 50 or 100 years. Between 1851 and 1900, 31 species of mammals and many species of birds became extinct. Street says that 44 species of mammals and probably an equal number or more of avian species have been extinguished or allowed to die out since 1800. Herein lies the unnaturalness of recent extinctions.

All animals are infinitely complex organisms, and each one is an intricate and valuable link in the chain of existence. Man is an animal enthralled

The cheetah has been hunted by man and has become an endangered species. The extinction of a species is not a modern phenomenon. It is the accelerated pace at which species die out now that concerns conservationists. Man can erase millions of years of evolution by lack of restraint in his predation.

by his own powers. Recently, he has disregarded or discarded some species that seem to be of little value or direct use to him. It is now essential for man to see nature as dynamically balanced in a pattern of cycles. He must replace his view of evolution that puts him at the top of a ladder of progress with one that permits him to see his own vulnerability and strength in relation to the existence of all other species.

GLOSSARY

∝-male
one of the dominant males in a troop of animals; usually lead the group movements; may take primary role in group defense and priority in mating.

Agnatha
jawless fish; some of these are representatives of the earliest vertebrates; modern forms include hagfish and lamprey.

amphibians
a class of vertebrates which can breathe and move on land but which must spawn their eggs in water; poikilothermic; scaleless skin.

anthropoid
a member of one of the two suborders of the Primate order; a monkey, ape, or man.

autotroph
an organism that manufactures its own food from materials in the environment; plants are autotrophs.

baleen
whalebone; the whalebone blades that hang from the roof of a whale's mouth and catch plankton as seawater rushes through the whale's mouth as it closes its jaws.

benthic
living at the bottom of deep seas.

bipedal
walking and standing on hindlimbs.

Boidae (boid)
a snake family; a member of the snake family that includes pythons, boa constrictors and anacondas. They are non-poisonous.

carnassials
bladelike premolar and molar teeth of carnivores.

carrion
the decaying flesh of a carcass.

cervical
pertaining to the neck or neck-like structures.

chemoreceptor
nerve cells able to detect molecules diffused in gas or liquid; smell or taste receptor.

Chiroptera
the bat family.

Chondricthyes
fish with cartilaginous skeletons.

conspecifics
members of the same species.

dimorphic
that which has two forms or shapes.

dorsal
of, on or near the back.

dynes/cm²
the dyne is a unit of force that can accelerate one gram of matter one centimeter per second. Dynes per square centimeter show how many units of force of this magnitude there are over a given surface area.

ecological niche
an environmental zone, composed of substrate, climate, and occupant species.

exogenous
that which originates or develops outside the organism; external influence upon the organism as opposed to that which arises within the organism itself; that which exerts its influence upon the organism from outside.

fossorial
habitually living and moving about underground.

genome
the genetic makeup of an organism.

gonad
the sex gland of an organism; where the gametes (ova and spermatozoa) are produced.

gregarious
habitually living in groups, flocks, herds, clusters, troops or colonies.

herbivore
an animal that eats plants primarily.

hermaphrodite
organism that possesses gonads of both sexes, either simultaneously or at different stages in ontogeny.

herptiles
amphibians and reptiles collectively.

heterotroph
an organism that eats other organisms.

homeothermy
maintaining a constant temperature.

Hominidae (hominid)
the family of man, including species of the genera *Ramapithecus*, *Australopithecus*, and *Homo*; a member of this family.

idiomorphic
a genus whose members have similar appearances and body types.

Insectivora
an order of mammals having species that are thought to be similar to primitive eutherian mammals; eat insects primarily, e.g. hedgehogs, tenrecs, shrews.

maxillary
referring to the upper jaw.

metamorphosis
process of changing shape and appearance.

Mysticeti
the baleen whales, like blue and sei.

nasal plug
in whales, the front end of the windpipe that fits into the lower end of the blowhole passage and prevents water from entering lungs during a dive.

neurotransmitter
a chemical substance that enables electrical impulses to cross the gaps between nerve cells.

Odontoceti
the toothed whales, like killer and narwhal.

ontogenetic (ontogeny)
lifetime; life history or development.

Osteicthyes
bony fishes.

oviparous
animals whose fertilized eggs develop outside of the mother's body.

ovoviparous
animals whose fertilized eggs develop in the oviducts or body cavity of mother; embryos are nourished on yolk alone, not maternal tissues.

pelagic
of the sea; living in the open sea; oceanic, not coastal.

Pinnipedia
a suborder of the order of Carnivora, including seals, walrus, and sea lion.

poikilothermic
having a body temperature that varies with environmental temperature.

phylogenetic (phylogeny)
of the lifetime of a group of animals, usually the life history of a species; the evolutionary development of a species.

phytoplankton
microscopic and small scale plant life in water.

polymorphic
a genus whose members have many different appearances and body types.

pygopodidae
flap-footed lizards of Australia and New Guinea; snake-like reptiles without forelegs and with hindlimbs reduced to small flaps of skin.

Primates
the order of mammals to which prosimians, monkeys, apes and man belong.

primitive
that which has not evolved (or changed) much through time.

protandric
a hermaphrodite (fish) that is male first and female at a later point in its development.

protogynic
a hemaphrodite (fish) that is female first and male at a later point in its development.

reptiles
the first class of vertebrates that could live on land exclusively; poikilothermic; calcerous-shelled eggs laid on land; scales cover body.

savanna
a grassy plain with few trees.

selachian
the collective name for all species of sharks, skates and rays.

sexually dimorphic
the characteristic of body size, build and behaviour differences between the sexes of a species.

specialized
that which has undergone many evolutionary changes and is adapted to very specific environmental or behavioral requirements.

spp.
abbreviation for species (plural).

steppe
level temperate zone tracts of land in central Asia and south-eastern Europe and the USSR.

sutures
irregular junctions between skull bones.

taxonomy
classification of plants and animals by their similarities of structure and behavior.

Teleosti
bony fishes.

terrestrial
habitually living and moving about on land.

ventral
belly side.

ventricle (brain)
space filled with cerebrospinal fluid.

vertebrates
animals having a segmented, bony column supporting and surrounding the spinal cord.

viable
that which is functional, workable, fertile.

viviparous
animals whose fertilized eggs develop in the mother's body and are nourished by maternal tissues.

zooplankton
microscopic and small scale animal life in water.

INDEX

BIBLIOGRAPHY

Brown, L. *African Birds of Prey*. Houghton Mifflin. 1971.

Cousteau, J. Y. and Diole, P. *The Whale, Mighty Monarch of the Sea*. Doubleday. 1972.

Eaton, R. L. *The Cheetah*. Van Nostrand Rheingold Co. 1974.

Eimeil, S. and DeVore, I. *The Primates* Time-Life. 1971.

Gans, C. *Reptiles of the World*. Bantam. 1975.

Goin, C. J. and Goin, O. B. *Introduction to Herpetology*. Freeman and Co. 1962.

Gordon, S. *Days with the Golden Eagle*. Williams and Norgate. 1927.

Harrison-Matthews, L. *The Whale*. Simon and Schuster. 1968.

Hausman, L. A. *Birds of Prey*. Smith. 1966.

Hvass, H. *Fishes of the World*. Dutton. 1965.

Griffin, D. R. *Listening in the Dark*. Dover. 1958.

Isemonger, R. M. *Snakes of Africa*. Nelson. 1962.

Keiffer, E. 'Sharks', *New York Times Magazine*. May 4, 1975.

Kruuk, H. *The Spotted Hyena*. University of Chicago Press. 1972.

Lagler, K. F., Bardach, J. E. and Miller, R. E. *Icthyology*. University of Michigan Press. 1962.

Lorenz, K. *On Aggression*. Bantam. 1966.

Macdonald, J. D., Goodwin, D. and Adler, H. E., *Bird Behavior*. Sterling. 1962.

McCormick, H. W. and Allen, T. *Shadows in the Sea*. Chilton. 1963. (M & A)

Mech, L. D. *The Wolf: The Ecology and Behavior of an Endangered Species*. Natural History Press. 1970.

Minton, S. A., and Minton, M. R. *Venomous Reptiles*. Scribners Sons. 1969.

Mohr, C. E., and Poulson, T. L. *Life of the Cave*. McGraw-Hill. 1966.

Morris, R., and Morris, D. *Men and Snakes*. McGraw-Hill. 1965.

Neill, W. T. *The Last of the Ruling Reptiles*. Columbia University Press. 1971.

Oliver, J. A. *The Natural History of North American Amphibians and Reptiles*. Van Nostrand Co. 1955.

Gano, C. and Parsons, T. S. (eds.) *Biology of the Reptilia*. Academic Press. 1970.

Pope, C. H. *The Giant Snakes*. Knopf. 1961.

Roots, C. *Animals of the Dark*. Praeger. 1974.

Schaller, G. B. *Serengeti: A Kingdom of Predators*. Knopf. 1972.

Scheffer, V. B. *The Year of the Whale*. Scribners Sons. 1969.

Schaller, G. B. *The Deer and the Tiger*. University of Chicago Press. 1967.

Snyder, N., and Snyder, H. 'Feather and Fury: the Cooper's Hawk'. *National Geographic*. March 1974. pp. 432–442.

Sylva de, D. P. *Great Barracuda*. V. Miami Press. 1963. *Studies in Tropical Oceanography* No. 1. October 1963.

Tinbergen, N. *The Study of Instinct*. Oxford University Press. 1974.

Tyne, J. Van and Berger, A. J. *Fundamentals of Ornithology*. Wiley and Sons. 1959.

Vaughan, T. A. *Mammology*. Saunders. 1972.

PICTURE CREDITS